Pizza & Wine

PIZZA & WINE

AUTHENTIC ITALIAN RECIPES AND WINE PAIRINGS

LEONARDO CURTI AND JAMES O. FRAIOLI

FOOD PHOTOGRAPHY AND STYLING BY JESSICA NICOSIA-NADLER
LIFESTYLE PHOTOGRAPHY BY MEAGAN SZASZ

GIBBS SMITH
TO ENRICH AND INSPIRE HUMANKIND
Salt Lake City | Charleston | Santa Fe | Santa Barbara

First Edition
13 12 11 10 09   5 4 3 2 1

Text © 2009 Leonardo Curti and James O. Fraioli
Food Photography © 2009 Jessica Nicosia-Nadler
Lifestyle Photography © 2009 Meagan Szasz
Wood-Fired Oven Photography © 2009 Mugnaini Inc. pages 4, 14, 16, 17,
    18, 27, 28, and 31
Additional Photography © 2009 Brian Hodges, pages 61, 147–149

Published by
Gibbs Smith
P.O. Box 667
Layton, Utah 84041

1-800.835.4993 orders
www.gibbs-smith.com

Designed and produced by Debra McQuiston
Printed and bound in Hong Kong
Gibbs Smith books are printed on either recycled, 100% post-consumer waste,
FSC-certified papers, or on paper produced from a 100% certified sustainable forest/
controlled wood source.

Library of Congress Cataloging-in-Publication Data
Curti, Leonardo.
  Pizza & wine : authentic Italian recipes and wine pairings / Leonardo
Curti and James O. Fraioli ; food photography and styling by Jessica
Nicosia-Nadler ; lifestyle photography by Meagan Szasz. — 1st ed.
    p. cm.
  Includes index.
  ISBN-13: 978-1-4236-0514-0
  ISBN-10: 1-4236-0514-4
  1. Pizza. 2. Wine and wine making. 3. Trattoria Grappolo (Santa Ynez,
Calif.) I. Fraioli, James O., 1968- II. Title.
  TX770.P58C87 2009
  641.8'24—dc22
                        2008054136

Pizza—*che delizioso!*

There's something irresistible about sinking our teeth into a fresh-baked crust smothered with rich tomato sauce and toasted, molten mozzarella, hot from the oven. Since Lombardi's of New York first introduced us to the Italian pie back at the turn of the century, America's love affair with pizza has grown. We now spend $32 billion a year satisfying our passion for pizza, seeking it out in hole-in-the-wall mom and pop pizzerias, calling for a movie-night-in delivery from all-American mega-chains like Domino's and Pizza Hut, and even finding it on menus of some of the trendiest upscale restaurants.

But the gusto and enthusiasm Americans bring to pizza have taken the dish far from its Italian roots. When it comes to toppings, we can't get enough. From double pepperoni to extra cheese to the "ultimate meat lover's" pizza piled high with half a dozen meats, we seem to have a super-sized appetite for colossal pizza pies. The chains have cooked up firmer crusts to carry the extra loads, Chicago developed its famous deep-dish pizza to hold it all, and New York devised a style of folding over giant slices to keep all the contents from spilling over.

Not so in Italy.

Two thousand years ago in the Mediterranean region, Italian cooks were baking flour dough on a large stone heated in the fire, achieving a crisp but fluffy flatbread. Eventually, wood-fired ovens replaced the open flame and hot stones. Using such ovens, the Neapolitans created what many pizza aficionados to this day consider the quintessential pizza: a soft thin crust lightly charred from wood-oven baking and infused with smoky flavor, brushed sparingly with a long-simmered tomato sauce made from the ripest of Italian tomatoes, topped with a sprinkling of fresh mozzarella cheese and finished—immediately after the pie is pulled from the oven—with a few freshly torn basil leaves and a drizzle of extra virgin olive oil. For Italians, just as a pasta dish is more about the pasta than the sauce, Italian pizza is about the crust. The toppings are always savory and delicious, but they are also few and never overwhelming.

In keeping with the spirit and soul of these Italian traditions, we are excited to introduce our latest cookbook: *Pizza & Wine: Authentic Italian Recipes and Wine Pairings*. In the delightful pages ahead, we will take you step by step through making your own remarkable Neapolitan style crust—crunchy at

the rim, thin and moist in the middle, yet light enough to pair perfectly with whatever toppings you choose.

And we certainly have not forgotten the toppings. Our goal with the recipes in this book is to not only give you some incredibly tasty combinations to try, but also to inspire your own creativity—a perfect Neapolitan crust is a canvas awaiting your culinary artistry. To get you started, Chef Leonardo offers the *Traditional Margherita* pizza—tomato, basil, and cheese—plus many other mouthwatering pies such as *Roman Artichoke with Capers and Shaved Parmesan, Poached Pear with Gorgonzola and Speck, Pancetta with White Asparagus,* and *Lobster with Ripe Avocado and Cherry Tomatoes.* As a tip-of-the-hat to non-Italians like Wolfgang Puck, whose creative toppings have for years pushed pizza lovers to think outside the box, Chef Leonardo has included a variation on the *Smoked Salmon with Caviar and Chive* pizza. And to complement the delicious pies you'll soon be making, he has also tossed in some delicious appetizers, breads, and desserts to complete your pizza-dining experience.

For those who have yet to add a wood-fired oven to their kitchen or backyard, rest assured that all the pizzas in this book can be made in a conventional oven using a preheated pizza stone, or even on the grill. However, we urge you to at least start dreaming of a wood-fired oven of your own. We truly believe these ovens are the best-kept secret in culinary America. Not only are they an exciting and fun way to cook, they are extremely versatile and bring style, sophistication, and beauty to any indoor or outdoor kitchen. They inevitably become the focal point whenever you entertain and add a festive but homey atmosphere to any gathering of family and friends.

Without question, a critical part of any wood-fired oven is the firebrick floor—it must have just the right porosity to allow the raw dough to steam off into the tiles and allow the high temperatures of approximately 750 degrees F

to quickly move up through the pizza. This is what produces that perfect crust—soft in the center and blistered and charred around the rim. The superior cooking floor of the Mugnaini wood-fired oven stands as the benchmark others try to achieve. Mugnaini ovens are handcrafted by Refratarri Valoriani, the same family of artisans that have been making wood-fired ovens since 1890. The tradition started when Sylvio Valoriani patented his wood-fired oven design in Italy in 1946. This elegant solution made oven ownership possible for everyone and is still the standard for wood-fired ovens worldwide. Mugnaini ovens are actually a hybrid of the Valoriani oven and use their residential dome and commercial-grade floor for a unique combination that results in fast start-up times with professional results. This creates an oven ideal for the way we wish to cook today. Thanks to Andrea Mugnaini and Mugnaini Imports, Mugnaini ovens come in a variety of sizes and styles, and are finding their way into more and more homes across America.

Of course, no Italian meal—and that includes pizza—is complete without a glass of fine wine. When pairing a wine, simply focus on the toppings. True, the crust is critical to the pizza, but (like bread) *all* wines go well with it. So, it is the toppings that should be considered in pairing. For instance, light meatless pizzas like Chef Leonardo's *Roasted Potato with White Truffle Oil* do exceptionally well with a crisp Chardonnay, while his *Fresh Strawberry and Mascarpone* pizza will make a fine Champagne wake up and sing. We've offered pairing suggestions for all the pizzas and appetizers in this book, but a good rule of thumb to remember is that relatively simple, fruit-driven, soft-textured wines—red or white—usually do best with pizza. But—as with the new topping combinations we hope this book will inspire you to create—the fun is in the testing.

Buono appetito!

—Chef Leonardo Curti and James O. Fraioli

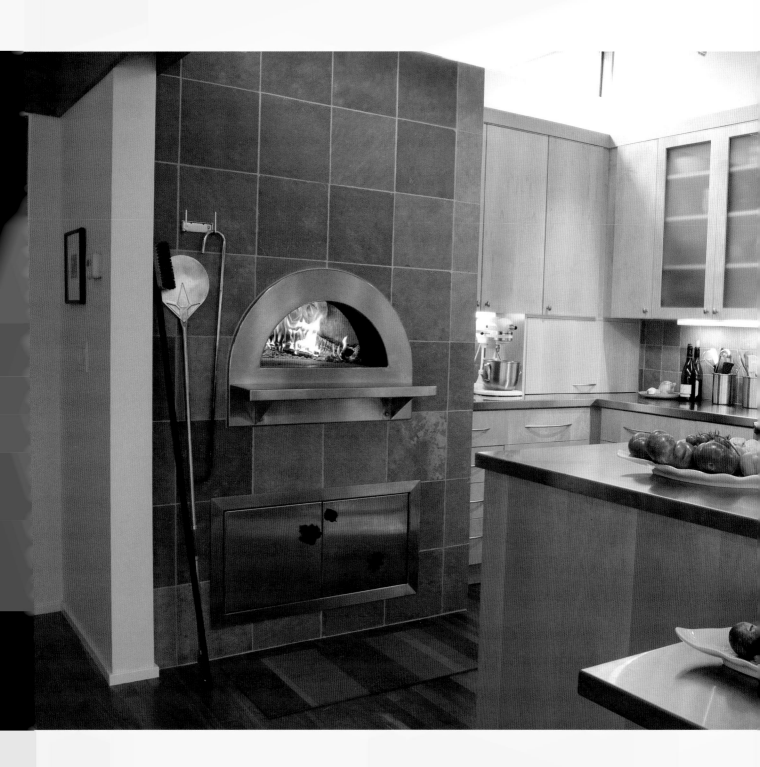

THE WOOD-FIRED OVEN

With no moving parts, save for the door, the wood-fired oven is the simplest as well as most versatile appliance in any indoor or outdoor kitchen. The range of heat is higher than what conventional ovens can reach, and cooking with a live flame helps the home chef create delightful dishes impossible in any other oven. Wood-fired ovens are perfect for creating delicious home-made pizzas.

HEAT

The wood-fired oven utilizes three types of heat to produce superior results. *(This information is courtesy of the Mugnaini Wood-Fired Cooking School.)*

1. Conductive heat—offered by the firebrick floor. Breads and pizzas are placed directly onto the floor to bake, but almost any type of cookware can be used in the same way you would cook on a stovetop. The deep, even heat of the floor tiles is infinitely adjustable by simply moving the pan in relationship to the fire.

2. Radiant heat—provided by the dome. The fierce energy of the fire is absorbed by the clay dome and stored for hours of cooking, then softly radiates throughout the entire cooking chamber. This heat is available whether the fire is going or not.

3. Convection flow of heat—created by the shape of the dome and the live fire placed on the side of the oven. This flow of heat circulating around the oven creates an incredibly balanced cooking chamber. By regulating the size of the flame, you can change the intensity of the oven.

NECESSARY TOOLS

Like handy tools used in the kitchen or at the outdoor grill, a wood-fired oven has its own specialized gadgets to make cooking safe, efficient, and fun. Here's a list of items to get you started. All of these and more can be found at *www.mugnaini.com*.

Dough Cutter: A knife will do, but when making pizza dough for a large pizza party, this handy device will quickly slice through pizza dough, saving you time so you can move on to more important things.

Dough Box: Be prepared for your next pizza party! These easy-to-carry plastic dough boxes are self-stacking and require only one lid. Each box holds about 15 dough balls, and not only are they a great space saver, but they will protect your fresh dough from drying out.

Infrared Thermometer: One of these remarkable gadgets will let you know the internal temperature of your wood-fired oven. For consistent and repeatable results in wood-fired cooking, you will always reference the "floor temperature" and not the ambient air temperature. The only way to accurately measure the various surface temperatures of the cooking floor is with a handheld infrared thermometer specifically designed for wood-fired ovens.

Ash Scraper: This is another must-have item. With its long handle and curved blade, the ash scraper safely moves the hot coals to properly position them for baking pizzas or cleaning your oven.

Wire-Brush: Like the ash scraper, this long-handled tool is essential for preparing and cleaning the wood-fired oven.

Cookware (bakers, casseroles, pots, saucepans, etc): Terra cotta is one of the oldest and most durable materials used for quality cookware. Terra cotta cookware prevents evaporation of sauces and juices so your foods stay moist during cooking. They are also lead free and dishwasher safe. We recommend acquiring a few different sizes and shapes for all of your cooking needs.

Pizza Peel: The quintessential device for sliding pizzas in and out of the wood-fired oven. They come in various sizes, with short and long handles. Peels (or paddles to some) are made from commercial stainless steel to solid wood. Pick up a couple and see what works best for you. We recommend making the pizzas directly on a short-handle wooden peel, sliding the pizza in the oven, then using a long metal peel with a small round, flat head to rotate the pizza once it's in the oven to evenly brown the edges.

Pizza Cutter: This handheld tool cuts perfect and professional pizza slices for your family and friends to enjoy. We recommend purchasing a cutter with a large wheel—making the slicing process much easier.

LIGHTING, HEATING, AND COOKING

Lighting and heating a wood-fired oven is a very simple process. First, the fire should be built in the middle of the oven. Start with a fire starter. We like to use Weber fire starters. They are food grade and offer about 10 minutes of flame. Light the starters and once they are aflame, add some kindling and three or four pieces of double-split seasoned hardwood (any hardwood is fine). Within minutes, you will have an established fire. Should the fire die out at any time during the lighting process, simply add more fire starters and/or kindling. Old wine barrels, if you can get your hands on them, also make great—and flavorful—wood for burning.

Let the wood burn, adding additional pieces depending on how much cooking you intend to do. Once the desired amount of wood is determined, let the wood burn down to coals. At this stage, it is time to push the fire to one side of the oven and burn until any residual black smoke disappears off the dome. To do so, use an ash scraper—a long-handle stainless-steel tool designed for wood-fired ovens—to safely move the hot coals. Naturally

you will be adding wood to keep the fire going. The timing is a matter of several factors, but you must burn the black off of the dome on one side before you move the fire over to the other side.

Once the dome is preheated (void of black), you will have established a glowing bed of coals that you can regulate for different cooking environments by simply adding wood. For a pizza oven environment, we like to have the flame rolling across the top of the dome and a floor temperature of 650 to 750 degrees F. The floor temperature is best measured with a handheld infrared thermometer. For this style of cooking you will be adding one to two small pieces of wood about every 20 minutes.

For roasting, we first bring the oven up to pizza temperature and then let the fire die down so the flame is just rolling up the side of the oven. Most roasting is done in the 550 to 600 degrees F range with just a little live fire. It is very effective to start with a higher temperature and let the oven drop slightly or even place the door on the front after the flame dies out completely. Cook times are based on the internal temperature of your food rather than a time and temperature formula. If the oven floor temperature drops, just add a piece of hardwood. And always keep fire starters and some kindling on hand in case you need to reestablish the fire.

For baking, we also bring the oven up to pizza temperature to ensure deep even heat, but we let the fire die down completely and the oven cool off to 450 degrees F. This works wonderfully for lasagna, casseroles, and desserts like fruit tarts or apple crisps. The door can be closed all the way to hold in the heat; however, if there is any live flame, a smoky flavor could be imparted. Either leave the door slightly open or wait for the fire to die down completely.

For baking or roasting, aluminum foil tents work great to keep the top from browning too quickly. If you need more color, remove the foil or burn a little kindling for more browning. Also remember the oven is hottest next to the fire, so trust your senses and move your dish closer to the fire for more heat or away from the fire if it is too hot.

With a little attention to detail, the task of heating an oven will bring an oven up to temperature quickly and evenly. You then will be able to regulate the oven into the three distinct cooking environments by monitoring the size of the flame.

CLEANING

Cleaning a wood-fired oven is a simple process, similar to cleaning out a fireplace.

When the oven has completely cooled, use an ash scraper to move the pile of ash and coals to the front of the oven. With a dust pan and brush, shovel the contents into a bucket or garbage sack for safe removal.

With a long-handled bristle brush designed for wood-fired ovens, sweep the fine ash particles off the oven floor and discard.

We also like to clean and sanitize the oven before every use. To do so, simply toss a handful of coarse rock salt in the oven. Next, wrap a towel around your wood-fired brush and gently scrub the salt around the floor tiles. When the salt has dissolved, your oven is clean and ready for use.

ESSENTIALS

Pizza making begins

with two essential recipes. Most everyone will agree that when it comes to pizza, there's nothing better than a homemade crust and an authentic Italian pizza sauce. The following two recipes will help create the base for exceptional pizzas every time.

FRESH PIZZA DOUGH

MAKES 6 (10-INCH) PIZZAS

1 package dry active yeast
2 cups Italian natural spring water (bottled and still, such as Sole)
2 teaspoons sea salt
6 cups all-purpose Italian flour
2 tablespoons extra virgin olive oil

IN AN ELECTRIC mixer with the dough hook attached, stir yeast and lukewarm water until combined. Add salt and flour until dough begins to form and is not sticky, about 10 to 12 minutes.

PLACE DOUGH IN a bowl that has been lightly coated with oil. Coat the entire dough ball with oil as well. Cover bowl with plastic wrap and let dough rise in a warm place for about 1 hour.

REMOVE DOUGH FROM bowl and place on a smooth working surface. Divide the dough into 6 balls, about 6 to 7 ounces each. Place each dough ball on a lightly floured surface and cover with a towel. Let rise about 45 minutes.

ONE AT A time, roll each dough ball on a floured surface until a thin 10-inch round pizza shape is formed. Store extra dough balls by simply freezing in plastic wrap.

HOMEMADE PIZZA SAUCE

MAKES ABOUT 2 CUPS

2 cups Italian tomato purée
2 tablespoons extra virgin
olive oil
Dash of dried oregano
1 clove garlic, peeled
and smashed
Sea salt to taste

IN A BLENDER, add all of the ingredients and puree until combined. Store in refrigerator until ready to use.

FOCACCIAS, APPETIZERS, & SIDE DISHES

Before we delve into the

the pizzas themselves, let's talk briefly about starter courses and side dishes. Depending on the size of your gathering, you should serve at least two appetizers before and during the pizza making process. You can add another while the pizza is coming out of the oven. This allows family, friends and guests to relax and enjoy without feeling compelled to snack on the irresistible pizza toppings being prepped on the counter.

The following recipes are all simple to make and pair extremely well with pizza. Serving a tantalizing focaccia topped with melted cheese and herbs immediately readies the palate for the texture of fresh-baked pizza dough soon to

be consumed. A savory spread made with hand-packed anchovy fillets—an Italian pantry essential—on toasted bread will no doubt whisk guests off to the Mediterranean, if only for a short while. Traditional Italian tarts and pastries filled with dried cod, artichokes, and sausage are other exquisite delicacies that should be sampled and savored, particularly on cold winter nights. The same holds true for Chef Leonardo's *Baked Mussels* on the half shell.

During hot summer months, when outdoor entertaining seems to be in full swing, certain foods have the ability of conjuring up images of crashing waves and salty sea breezes amidst white sandy beaches. On such occasions, try serving *Bacon-Wrapped Sea Scallops with Fennel and Fava Beans,* crisp and refreshing *Swordfish Carpaccio with Orange, Grapefruit, and Fennel Salad,* or a generous helping of *Panzanella*—an authentic Tuscan bread salad made with fresh herbs, vegetables, and tuna fish.

Whatever starter combination you choose to serve your guests, one thing is for certain: everyone will be pleasantly satisfied as they eagerly await one of the world's most popular foods—pizza!

FOCACCIA WITH BASIL

MAKES 2 LOAVES

1 package dry active yeast
1½ cups warm water
½ cup extra virgin olive oil
2 pounds flour (or 8 cups)
½ tablespoon salt
Sea salt to taste
2 tablespoons fresh minced basil

DISSOLVE THE YEAST in warm water until foamy and then add the oil. Sift the flour and salt together into the bowl of an electric mixer with a dough hook attached. Turn on low speed and add the yeast mixture. Work for about 15 minutes to obtain a smooth and elastic dough. Divide the dough into two pieces, and then place them individually into an oiled bowl and cover with plastic wrap; set aside. Allow the dough to double in size. After the dough has risen, remove each piece from bowl and work by stretching the dough into a shallow wood-fired oven-proof baking pan and punching it down with your fingertips. Top with a sprinkle of sea salt, basil, and drizzle with olive oil. Allow the dough to double in size.

PLACE PANS INTO the wood-fired oven when the temperature has cooled to around 400 degrees F and bake for about 45 to 55 minutes. If using a conventional oven, preheat to 400 degrees F and bake about 1 hour or until golden brown.

WHEAT FOCACCIA WITH ASIAGO CHEESE

MAKES 2 LOAVES

1 package dry active yeast
1½ cups warm water
½ cup extra virgin olive oil
2 pounds wheat flour (or 8 cups)
½ tablespoon salt
½ cup grated Asiago cheese
Sea salt to taste

DISSOLVE THE YEAST in warm water until foamy and then add the oil. Sift the flour and salt together into the bowl of an electric mixer with a dough hook attached. Turn on low speed and add the yeast mixture. Work for about 15 minutes to obtain a smooth and elastic dough. Divide the dough into two pieces, and then place them individually into an oiled bowl and cover with plastic wrap; set aside. Allow the dough to double in size. After the dough has risen, remove each piece from bowl and work by stretching the dough into a shallow wood-fired oven-proof baking pan and then punching it down with your fingertips. Sprinkle sea salt on top along with the Asiago cheese and drizzle with olive oil. Allow the dough to double in size.

PLACE PANS INTO the wood-fired oven when the temperature has cooled to around 400 degrees F and bake for about 45 to 55 minutes. If using a conventional oven, preheat to 400 degrees F and bake about 1 hour or until golden brown.

ANCHOVIES ON ITALIAN TOAST

SERVES 4

2 cloves garlic
10 hand-packed anchovy fillets
1 tablespoon white truffle oil
2 tablespoons fresh chopped
Italian parsley
4 tablespoons porcini mushrooms
in oil, drained
4 slices country bread
¼ cup butter, melted

IN A CUISINART or blender, blend the garlic, anchovies, truffle oil, parsley, and mushrooms until a paste consistency is achieved. Meanwhile, toast the bread in the wood-fired pizza oven (or under the broiler if using a conventional oven) until lightly brown. Remove from heat and top each slice with the anchovy mixture. Return to heat to warm and then remove. Drizzle each slice with melted butter and serve warm.

RUSACK CHARDONNAY, SANTA BARBARA COUNTY

The grapes for this Chardonnay hail from two cool climate appellations within the county—the Bien Nacido and Goodchild vineyards in the Santa Maria Valley, and Rancho Santa Rosa in the Santa Rita Hills. The blending for this wine has resulted in a marriage of exceptional fruit aromas with carefully balanced acidity. Honeydew melon, Asian pear, orange blossom, and ample citrus notes are highlighted in this appealingly crisp white wine.

PUFF PASTRY WITH DRIED COD AND ARTICHOKE

SERVES 4

1 pound dried cod, pre-soaked and diced
¼ cup olive oil
2 cloves garlic, crushed
Sea salt and black pepper to taste
¼ cup dry white wine
5 Roman artichoke hearts,
separated into pieces
4 tablespoons fresh chopped
Italian parsley
1 sheet puff pastry
Egg wash (a combination of
2 eggs and 2 tablespoons
milk beaten together)

PARSLEY SAUCE

½ cup fresh Italian parsley (leaves only)
2 cloves garlic
Pinch of sea salt
Pinch of crushed red pepper
1 tablespoon fresh lemon juice
¼ cup extra virgin olive oil

SOAK THE DRIED cod in cold water for at least 18 hours and with at least three water changes over the 18-hour period.

IN A LARGE sauté pan, over medium-high heat, add the oil and garlic, and let cook until garlic is soft and golden. Add the salt, pepper, and wine. Add the artichoke hearts and cook about 5 to 7 minutes. Remove from heat, dice the cod, and add along with the parsley; mix well. Spread the mixture onto a rolled-out sheet of puff pastry. After the mixture is evenly spread, roll the puff pastry and then brush the finished roll with egg wash.

PLACE IN THE wood-fired oven after it has cooled down to around 395 degrees F and bake for 20 minutes or until golden brown. Follow same temperature and time settings if using a conventional oven. Serve hot with a side of parsley sauce.

TO MAKE THE sauce, pulse the parsley, garlic, salt, red pepper, and lemon juice in a Cuisinart or blender. Slowly add the oil until the mixture is well combined. Store in refrigerator until ready to use.

F I O R E

FIORE SANGIOVESE, SANTA YNEZ VALLEY

The fruit of Sangiovese hails from the eastern area of the Santa Ynez Valley in Santa Barbara County. The conditions of this area, climate and soils, reflect the agriculture environment of Tuscany allowing the fruit to be generous with perfect clusters, excellent color, and beaming with flavor. Enjoy flavors of cherry and spice fruit with rich tannins and silky textures.

ARTICHOKE AND ITALIAN SAUSAGE TART

SERVES 4

¼ cup olive oil
4 green onions, sliced
6 baby artichoke hearts, diced
Salt and pepper to taste
2 anchovy fillets
2 mild Italian sausages, casings removed and crumbled
2 sheets puff pastry
½ cup milk
2 eggs
¼ cup grated fresh Parmesan cheese
Egg wash (a combination of 2 eggs and 2 tablespoons milk beaten together)

IN A SAUTÉ pan over medium-high heat, add the oil and onions and cook until onions are soft. Add the artichoke hearts, salt, and pepper; cover and continue to cook for about 4 to 5 minutes. Add the anchovies and crumbled sausage. Continue to cook until the sausage is cooked thoroughly. Remove from heat and let cool. Place one sheet of puff pastry in a 12-inch wood-fired ovenproof pie pan. Fill the pan with the artichoke and sausage mixture.

IN A SEPARATE bowl, whisk the milk, eggs, and cheese together. Pour the liquid over the artichoke and sausage mixture. Cut the other puff pastry sheet into strips and place in a crisscross pattern over the top.

BRUSH WITH THE egg wash, place in the oven after it has cooled down to about 350 degrees F, and bake for 15 to 20 minutes or until golden brown. If using a conventional oven, use the same temperature and time setting.

KYNSI ZINFANDEL, WEST RIVER, BARN OWL VINEYARDS

Kynsi is a small family winery located in San Luis Obispo's Edna Valley on the south central California coast. Grapes for this wine were sourced from the The Barn Owl Vineyard located on the west side of Paso Robles. This limited production wine will give you a sense of raspberry jam, dried thyme with accents of red plums, and boysenberry. You may also sense a little white pepper on the finish.

BACON-WRAPPED SEA SCALLOPS WITH FENNEL AND FAVA BEANS

SERVES 6

6 large day-boat sea scallops
6 slices thick country bacon
6 stems dried fennel
(oregano or rosemary
stems may also be used)
¼ cup extra virgin olive oil
½ yellow onion, finely chopped
2 cloves garlic, minced
1 pound fresh (or frozen)
fava beans, in shell
1 tablespoon fennel seed
Sea salt and white pepper to taste
Chicken stock, optional
Pinch of crushed red pepper
Citrus oil

WASH AND PAT dry the sea scallops and then wrap each scallop with 1 slice of bacon. Secure the bacon to the scallop with a dried stem of fennel; set aside.

IN A SAUTÉ pan over medium-high heat, add the oil, onion, and garlic, and cook until onion and garlic are soft. Add the fava beans and fennel seed (NOTE: If using frozen fava beans, completely thaw in cold water before using). Cook about 20 minutes, or until soft. Add salt, pepper, and crushed red pepper. If the mixture is too dry, moisten with a little chicken stock. Once beans are cooked, mash with a fork until smooth; set aside and keep warm.

IN THE WOOD-FIRED oven, or on an open grill, sear the scallops for about 3 minutes, turn over, and sear another 3 minutes. Remove the scallops from the heat.

TO SERVE, SCOOP a spoonful of the fava beans on the center of each plate and top with a seared scallop. Finish with a drizzle of citrus oil.

FALCONE FAMILY VINEYARDS CABERNET SAUVIGNON, PASO ROBLES

With an electric green-gold hue, this wine has an elusive and fresh aromatic array of saline, limes, lemon drops, lemon-lime margarita, green apple skin, white currants, and white apricots. Even more alluring are the other aspects of chalk, saltwater taffy, angel food cake, gingerbread, Italian parsley, and orange-flower blossom. In the mouth, the wine is ample and fleshy yet remains very chiseled, delineated, and crisp.

SWORDFISH CARPACCIO WITH ORANGE, GRAPEFRUIT, AND FENNEL SALAD

SERVES 4

Juice of 2 limes
¼ cup extra virgin olive oil
Pinch of sea salt and black pepper
8 paper-thin slices fresh swordfish
1 tablespoon fresh mint leaves
4 sprigs mint for garnish

SALAD

1 large orange, peeled and sliced
into bite-size wedges
1 large ruby red grapefruit, peeled
and sliced into bite-size wedges
1 small red onion, sliced
1 tablespoon red wine vinegar
1 fennel bulb, sliced
12 kalamata olives, pitted
4 tablespoons extra virgin olive oil
Sea salt and black pepper to taste

SQUEEZE THE LIME juice in a dish and add the oil, salt, and pepper. Gently lay the swordfish slices in the juice. Add the mint leaves and let sit about 15 to 20 minutes. Transfer to a serving plate and serve with the salad over top. Garnish each serving with a sprig of mint.

TO MAKE THE salad, combine the orange and grapefruit pieces, onion, vinegar, fennel, olives, oil, salt, and pepper in a bowl; mix well. Pour over swordfish slices along with the juice.

FULCRUM WINES PINOT NOIR, ANDERSON VALLEY

The fruit for this wine hails from the up-and-coming region of the Anderson Valley. Enjoy aromas of cherry, strawberry, rose, and violet with classic Anderson Valley earthiness. Bright cherry and berry fruit initially gives way to complex flavors of cola, nut, moss, and spice. The balanced acidity and seamlessly integrated tannins carry through to the long, smooth finish.

BAKED MUSSELS

SERVES 4

2 pounds fresh blue mussels,
debearded

¼ cup extra virgin olive oil

3 cloves garlic, chopped

½ cup Italian breadcrumbs

2 tablespoons chopped fresh
Italian parsley

Salt and pepper to taste

1 tablespoon grated fresh
Parmesan cheese

2 eggs

WASH AND CLEAN the mussels; set aside. Add the oil and garlic to a wood-fired ovenproof saucepan and place in the oven when the temperature has cooled to about 375 degrees F. When the pan is hot, add the mussels and cover and cook until they open. Remove from heat and set aside. (NOTE: To cook in a conventional oven, use the same temperature setting). Discard any unopen mussels and reserve the juice. When the mussels are cooled down, remove half of the shell and arrange in a baking dish with the meat side up.

IN A BOWL, add the reserved mussel juice, breadcrumbs, parsley, salt, pepper, and cheese. Mix well and pour over the mussels. Drizzle some oil on top and place in the oven to bake for about 10 minutes. While mussels are baking, whisk the eggs together. When the mussels are done, pour eggs over the mussels and bake an 10 minutes more. Serve warm.

JALAMA VINEYARD BY THE SEA PINOT NOIR, SANTA BARBARA COUNTY

The grapes for this wine come from the renowned Jalama Vineyard, the most western vineyard in Santa Barbara County. The vineyard is widely known for its hands-on farming techniques. The wine provides layers of black cherry. Plum and pomegranate also highlight this Santa Barbara County Pinot Noir. All the grapes are carefully selected by the winemaker to ensure a rich, ripe character that truly expresses the quality of the vineyard.

PANZANELLA

SERVES 4

4 Roma tomatoes, diced
1 cucumber, seeded and diced
4 anchovy fillets, chopped
1 red onion, diced
1 small bunch fresh basil,
julienned
1 tablespoon finely chopped fresh
Italian parsley
1 cup canned tuna in olive oil,
drained (about 8 ounces)
1 teaspoon dried oregano
Salt and pepper to taste
¼ cup red wine vinegar
8 slices ciabatta bread, dried
¼ cup extra virgin olive oil

IN A BOWL, add the tomatoes, cucumber, anchovies, onion, basil, parsley, tuna, oregano, salt, pepper, and vinegar; mix well. Lightly moisten the slices of bread with some cold water. Place the slices of moist bread in a baking dish and pour mixture over the bread. Refrigerate for up to 2 hours. Drizzle olive oil on top and serve.

**MAURITSON FAMILY WINERY
SAUVIGNON BLANC**

Bright pink grapefruit aromas are accented by dried apricot and fresh cut hay. The round texture in the mouth conjures flavors of honeydew melon and peach orchards. The lush yet vibrant mouthfeel gives way to clean balanced acidity in the back of the palate where the wine finishes with a hint of mineral.

VEGETARIAN PIZZAS

There isn't anything

better than fresh garden vegetables unless it's fresh garden vegetables on top of a homemade pizza! You can top your pizza with any herb or vegetable you like, and, depending on the season, you can make a light pizza for summer or a hearty pie for winter.

Whether you have your own garden, or simply purchase your veggies from the market, the most important element to consider when gathering pizza toppings is freshness. For recipes like Chef Leonardo's *Traditional Margherita* or *Quattro Formaggie*, always select fresh basil to enhance the taste and accentuate the delicious toppings. The same holds true for

the other ingredients you will use like fresh eggplant, garlic, red bell peppers, spinach, zucchini, zucchini blossoms, and even potatoes. Look for bright colors and ignore those vege-tables that are bruised or blemished. It is also best if you craft your vegetarian pizzas around whatever vegetables are in season. Often, the closer you are to the growing season, the fresher the produce and the better the taste. There are some pizza recipes that call for specific marinated vegetables. In these instances, purchase the marinated jar variety, such as capers, porcini mushrooms, artichoke hearts, and roasted red bell pepper (if you don't intend to make them yourself). These marinated veggies will add an extra kick to your homemade pizzas.

TRADITIONAL MARGHERITA

MAKES 1 (10-INCH) PIZZA

1 (6- to 7-ounce) ball fresh pizza
dough (see page 34)
½ cup homemade pizza sauce
(see page 35)
1 cup grated mozzarella cheese
6 to 8 fresh basil leaves
½ tablespoon dried oregano
Extra virgin olive oil

DUST A SMOOTH working surface with flour. Place pizza dough ball in the center. Flatten the dough into a disc shape with your fingers. Next, roll the dough with a rolling pin until it is thin and reaches a diameter of 10 to 12 inches. Spoon the sauce evenly over the top and sprinkle with the cheese.

USING A METAL or wood peel, place the pizza in the wood-fired oven, away from the fire, and let bake several minutes. Turn the pizza 180 degrees and continue baking another few minutes or until crust is golden brown and the cheese is bubbly. Remove pizza from the oven. Sprinkle basil leaves on top, along with the oregano and a drizzle of olive oil.

NOTE: IF USING a conventional oven, cook pizza at 450 degrees F on a preheated pizza stone on the middle oven rack.

CURTIS WINERY THE CROSSROAD, SANTA BARBARA VINEYARDS

The Crossroads is a distinctive blend of Grenache (75%) and Syrah (25%). Enjoy deep red fruit aromas with hints of cola and toasty oak. The palate is long and lively with bright flavors of strawberry cream, pomegranate, plum, and vanilla. Accents of peppery spice emerge on a juicy, harmonious finish.

magic

starts with fresh ingredients
like grilled zucchini and smoky
roasted peppers piled on generous
amounts of mozzarella cheese

ANCHOVY, MOZZARELLA, OLIVE OIL, OREGANO, AND TOMATO

MAKES 1 (10-INCH) PIZZA

1 (6- to 7-ounce) ball fresh pizza dough (see page 34)
½ cup homemade pizza sauce (see page 35)
1 cup grated mozzarella cheese
6 to 8 hand-packed anchovy fillets, drained (optional for vegetarians)
½ tablespoon dried oregano
Extra virgin olive oil

DUST A SMOOTH working surface with flour. Place pizza dough ball in the center. Flatten the dough into a disc shape with your fingers. Next, roll the dough with a rolling pin until it is thin and reaches a diameter of 10 to 12 inches. Spoon the sauce evenly over the top and sprinkle with the cheese. Slice the anchovy fillets in half, or keep whole, and arrange over the cheese, if using.

USING A METAL or wood peel, place the pizza in the wood-fired oven, away from the fire, and let bake several minutes. Turn the pizza 180 degrees and continue baking another few minutes or until crust is golden brown and the cheese is bubbly. Remove pizza from the oven. Sprinkle the oregano on top along with a drizzle of olive oil.

NOTE: IF USING a conventional oven, cook pizza at 450 degrees F on a preheated pizza stone on the middle oven rack.

PARAISO
———— ⬩ ————
SANTA LUCIA
HIGHLANDS

PARAISO VINEYARDS CHARDONNAY, SANTA LUCIA HIGHLANDS

Chardonnay from Monterey, and the Santa Lucia Highlands in particular, is all about balance. Ripe tropical fruit (pineapple, citrus, melon, apple) is teamed to rich viscosity, bright acidity, and a light overlay of vanillin oak. This famed "Paraiso Balance" gives this elegant wine myriad food-pairing possibilities.

QUATTRO FORMAGGIE

MAKES 1 (10-INCH) PIZZA

1 (6- to 7-ounce) ball fresh pizza dough (see page 34)
½ cup homemade pizza sauce (see page 35)
¼ cup grated Emmental cheese
¼ cup grated fontina cheese
¼ cup grated mozzarella cheese
¼ cup Gorgonzola cheese
6 to 8 fresh basil leaves
½ tablespoon dried oregano
Extra virgin olive oil

DUST A SMOOTH working surface with flour. Place pizza dough ball in the center. Flatten the dough into a disc shape with your fingers. Next, roll the dough with a rolling pin until it is thin and reaches a diameter of 10 to 12 inches. Spoon the sauce evenly over the top and sprinkle with the Emmental, fontina, and mozzarella cheeses. With your fingers, break the Gorgonzola into small pieces and arrange evenly over top.

USING A METAL or wood peel, place the pizza in the wood-fired oven, away from the fire, and let bake several minutes. Turn the pizza 180 degrees and continue baking another few minutes or until crust is golden brown and the cheese is bubbly. Remove pizza from oven. Sprinkle the fresh basil leaves on top, along with the oregano and a drizzle of olive oil.

NOTE: IF USING a conventional oven, cook pizza at 450 degrees F on a preheated pizza stone on the middle oven rack.

Consilience

CONSILIENCE WINES SYRAH, HAMPTON FAMILY VINEYARD

This is a very small production wine from the personal vineyard of one of the most well known vineyard managers in the central coast. Each grape is carefully plucked from the stem, held up and admired under a setting sun before being gently placed in the hopper . . . well, not really, but you get the idea. It's a Syrah that tends toward the dark fruit flavor spectrum with touches of blackberry and licorice, and nice chocolaty tannins.

EGGPLANT, ROASTED BELL PEPPER, AND ZUCCHINI

MAKES 1 (10-INCH) PIZZA

1 (6- to 7-ounce) ball fresh pizza dough (see page 34)
½ cup homemade pizza sauce (see page 35)
1 cup grated mozzarella cheese
4 slices fresh eggplant
8 slices fresh zucchini
Extra virgin olive oil
Salt and pepper
8 thin strips roasted red bell pepper*
½ tablespoon dried oregano

DUST A SMOOTH working surface with flour. Place pizza dough ball in the center. Flatten the dough into a disc shape with your fingers. Next, roll the dough with a rolling pin until it is thin and reaches a diameter of 10 to 12 inches. Spoon the sauce evenly over the top and sprinkle with the cheese; set aside.

TOSS THE EGGPLANT and zucchini in a small bowl with a drizzle of oil to coat and a pinch of salt and pepper. Transfer the vegetables to an outdoor grill, or inside the wood-fired oven, and cook until tender. Arrange the vegetables on the pizza along with the bell pepper.

USING A METAL or wood peel, place the pizza in the wood-fired oven, away from the fire, and let bake several minutes. Turn the pizza 180 degrees and continue baking another few minutes or until crust is golden brown and the cheese is bubbly. Remove pizza from oven. Sprinkle with the oregano and drizzle with olive oil.

NOTE: IF USING a conventional oven, cook pizza at 450 degrees F on a preheated pizza stone on the middle oven rack.

*THE RED BELL peppers can be purchased already roasted in a jar, or prepared at home. To roast a bell pepper, cut the pepper in half and remove seeds and membranes. Place peppers skin side up on an outdoor grill or inside the wood-fired oven until the skins are blackened. Immediately transfer the peppers to a paper bag and seal for about 10 minutes. Remove the peppers and peel off the skins. Slice into thin strips and toss with olive oil.

TRE ANELLI WINES SANGIOVESE, SANTA BARBARA COUNTY

Tre Anelli

Just acknowledging Sangiovese as the principal grape of Tuscany conjures up a vision in most people's minds of a place that one goes to get away. A place to eat well, a place to drink well, and a place to look out over the hills and think about the big picture. Of course it follows logically for Tre Anelli (sister winery to Consilience) that Sangiovese must be good for one's intellect, if not the soul, and assuages any guilt whatsoever about having that second glass.

ROASTED POTATO WITH WHITE TRUFFLE OIL

MAKES 1 (10-INCH) PIZZA

1 (6- to 7-ounce) ball fresh pizza
dough (see page 34)
1 cup grated mozzarella cheese
2 fresh Yukon gold potatoes
White truffle oil

DUST A SMOOTH working surface with flour. Place pizza dough ball in the center. Flatten the dough into a disc shape with your fingers. Next, roll the dough with a rolling pin until it is thin and reaches a diameter of 10 to 12 inches. Sprinkle with the cheese; set aside.

WASH AND DRY the potatoes. Slice each potato into thin potato chip–like slices, wrap in aluminum foil, and bake (either in a conventional oven, outdoor grill, or wood-fired oven) until tender. Remove from heat and discard foil. When cool, arrange on top of pizza.

USING A METAL or wood peel, place the pizza in the wood-fired oven, away from the fire, and let bake several minutes. Turn the pizza 180 degrees and continue baking another few minutes or until crust is golden brown and the cheese is bubbly. Remove pizza from oven. Drizzle with truffle oil.

NOTE: IF USING a conventional oven, cook pizza at 450 degrees F on a preheated pizza stone on the middle oven rack.

MELVILLE WINERY ESTATE CHARDONNAY, SANTA RITA HILLS

melville

With an electric green-gold hue, this wine has an elusive and fresh aromatic array of saline, limes, lemon drops, lemon-lime margarita, green apple skin, white currants, and white apricots. Even more alluring are the other aspects of chalk, saltwater taffy, angel food cake, gingerbread, Italian parsley, and orange-flower blossom. In the mouth, the wine is ample and fleshy yet remains very chiseled, delineated, and crisp.

BABY SPINACH WITH MOZZARELLA, PARMESAN CHEESE, AND GARLIC

MAKES 1 (10-INCH) PIZZA

1 (6- to 7-ounce) ball fresh pizza
dough (see page 34)
1/2 cup homemade pizza sauce
(see page 35)
1 cup grated mozzarella cheese
3 cups fresh baby spinach
4 to 6 cloves garlic, peeled
Extra virgin olive oil
Sea salt
1/4 cup grated Parmesan cheese

DUST A SMOOTH working surface with flour. Place pizza dough ball in the center. Flatten the dough into a disc shape with your fingers. Next, roll the dough with a rolling pin until it is thin and reaches a diameter of 10 to 12 inches. Spoon the sauce evenly over the top and sprinkle with the mozzarella cheese; set aside.

IN A SMALL pot, fill with salted water and boil over high heat. When boiling, add the spinach and let cook about 1 minute. Using a strainer or colander, drain the spinach, then press between two sheets of paper towels to extract any excess water. Add the wilted spinach to the pizza, along with the whole garlic cloves.

USING A METAL or wood peel, place the pizza in the wood-fired oven, away from the fire, and let bake several minutes. Turn the pizza 180 degrees and continue baking another few minutes or until crust is golden brown and the cheese is bubbly. Remove pizza from oven. Drizzle with olive oil and sprinkle sea salt and Parmesan cheese over top.

NOTE: IF USING a conventional oven, cook pizza at 450 degrees F on a preheated pizza stone on the middle oven rack.

WILDHURST VINEYARDS SAUVIGNON BLANC, LAKE COUNTY RESERVE

This light, refreshing wine is very typical of the Wildhurst-style Sauvignon Blanc. Enjoy grapefruit, fresh herbs, and gooseberry flavors. Crisp, fresh, and clean with plenty of tropical notes across the middle carrying the wine to a rich but steely finish.

ROMAN ARTICHOKE HEARTS WITH CAPERS AND GRATED PARMESAN CHEESE

MAKES 1 (10-INCH) PIZZA

1 (6- to 7-ounce) ball fresh pizza dough (see page 34)
½ cup homemade pizza sauce (see page 35)
1 cup grated mozzarella cheese
4 marinated Roman artichoke hearts
¼ cup grated Parmesan cheese
1 tablespoon capers
½ tablespoon dried oregano
Extra virgin olive oil

DUST A SMOOTH working surface with flour. Place pizza dough ball in the center. Flatten the dough into a disc shape with your fingers. Next, roll the dough with a rolling pin until it is thin and reaches a diameter of 10 to 12 inches. Spoon the sauce evenly over the top and sprinkle with the mozzarella cheese; crumble the artichoke hearts into pieces evenly over the top, or arrange whole.

USING A METAL or wood peel, place the pizza in the wood-fired oven, away from the fire, and let bake several minutes. Turn the pizza 180 degrees and continue baking another few minutes or until crust is golden brown. Remove pizza from oven. Sprinkle the Parmesan cheese on top, along with the capers, oregano, and a drizzle of olive oil.

NOTE: IF USING a conventional oven, cook pizza at 450 degrees F on a preheated pizza stone on the middle oven rack.

FOPPIANO VINEYARDS ESTATE PETITE SIRAH, RUSSIAN RIVER VALLEY

This Petite Sirah is made entirely from estate Petite Sirah grapes, grown on the family's Russian River Valley Estate. The wine is full-bodied and deeply colored. In the nose, the Petite offers black fruit aromas, which are well met on the palate with black and blue berry flavors, as well as toasty vanilla, exotic spices, and hints of cocoa on the finish.

EGGPLANT PARMESAN

MAKES 1 (10-INCH) PIZZA

1 (6- to 7-ounce) ball fresh pizza
dough (see page 34)
½ cup homemade pizza sauce
(see page 35)
1 cup grated mozzarella cheese
4 (¼-inch-thick) slices
fresh eggplant
Extra virgin olive oil
¼ cup grated Parmesan cheese
6–8 fresh basil leaves

DUST A SMOOTH working surface with flour. Place pizza dough ball in the center. Flatten the dough into a disc shape with your fingers. Next, roll the dough with a rolling pin until it is thin and reaches a diameter of 10 to 12 inches. Spoon the sauce evenly over the top and sprinkle generously with the mozzarella cheese; set aside.

ON A PLATE with flour, dust each slice of eggplant on both sides. Transfer to a sauté pan with 1 tablespoon olive oil over medium-high heat and pan fry for about 2 minutes on each side. Remove from heat and drain on paper towels. When cool, cut each eggplant slice in half and arrange on top of the pizza.

USING A METAL or wood peel, place the pizza in the wood-fired oven, away from the fire, and let bake several minutes. Turn the pizza 180 degrees and continue baking another few minutes or until crust is golden brown and the cheese is bubbly. Remove pizza from the oven. Sprinkle with Parmesan cheese and basil leaves and drizzle with olive oil.

NOTE: IF USING a conventional oven, cook pizza at 450 degrees F on a preheated pizza stone on the middle oven rack.

LUCAS & LEWELLEN MANDOLINA DOLCETTO

This early ripening grape, "little sweet one," produces a supple, elegant wine with medium body and mild tannins. Enjoy hints of dried cherry, oolong tea, and sage. This particular red wine is fermented cool to extract the blackberry, black cherry, tea, and tanned leather qualities. Aged for one year in French oak, Mandolina Dolcetto is a food-friendly wine.

PIZZA BIANCA WITH CHOPPED ROSEMARY, OLIVE OIL, AND SEA SALT

MAKES 1 (10-INCH) PIZZA

1 (6- to 7-ounce) ball fresh pizza dough (see page 34)
1 tablespoon chopped fresh rosemary
Sea salt
Extra virgin olive oil

DUST A SMOOTH working surface with flour. Place pizza dough ball in the center. Flatten the dough into a disc shape with your fingers. Next, roll the dough with a rolling pin until it is thin and reaches a diameter of 10 to 12 inches.

USING A METAL or wood peel, place the pizza in the wood-fired oven, away from the fire, and let bake several minutes. Turn the pizza 180 degrees and continue baking another few minutes or until crust is golden brown. Remove pizza from oven. Sprinkle the rosemary on top, along with a pinch of salt and a drizzle of olive oil.

NOTE: IF USING a conventional oven, cook pizza at 450 degrees F on a preheated pizza stone on the middle oven rack.

ARTHUR EARL WINERY CHARDONNAY, CENTRAL COAST

These grapes come from one of the warmer areas of California's central coast, producing a wine larger in flavor and with bigger mouthfeel. Aged in a mix of French and American oak, this Chardonnay bursts with full-flavored fruit and oak aromas that are well balanced and never overpowering.

ZUCCHINI BLOSSOMS WITH PARMESAN AND RICOTTA

MAKES 1 (10-INCH) PIZZA

1 (6- to 7-ounce) ball fresh pizza dough (see page 34)
½ cup homemade pizza sauce (see page 35)
1 cup grated mozzarella cheese
¼ cup ricotta cheese
6 to 8 fresh zucchini blossoms
¼ cup grated Parmesan cheese
Extra virgin olive oil

DUST A SMOOTH working surface with flour. Place pizza dough ball in the center. Flatten the dough into a disc shape with your fingers. Next, roll the dough with a rolling pin until it is thin and reaches a diameter of 10 to 12 inches. Spoon the sauce evenly over the top and sprinkle with the mozzarella cheese. Add dollops of ricotta cheese over top, along with the zucchini blossoms.

USING A METAL or wood peel, place the pizza in the wood-fired oven, away from the fire, and let bake several minutes. Turn the pizza 180 degrees and continue baking another few minutes or until crust is golden brown and the cheese is bubbly. Remove pizza from oven. Sprinkle the Parmesan cheese over top, along with a drizzle of olive oil.

NOTE: IF USING a conventional oven, cook pizza at 450 degrees F on a preheated pizza stone on the middle oven rack.

ALEXANDER & WAYNE PINOT GRIGIO, SANTA BARBARA COUNTY

These grapes come from the Los Alamos Valley, the middle of three transverse valleys in Santa Barbara County. The vines are among the oldest Italian plantings in the county and produce very Italian-style Pinot Grigios. This is a light, pleasant, easy drinking wine with plenty of fruit flavors complemented by the richness from the oak aging. Enjoy this one cold!

MARINATED PORCINI MUSHROOMS, TOMATO, MOZZARELLA, AND OLIVE OIL

MAKES 1 (10-INCH) PIZZA

1 (6- to 7-ounce) ball fresh pizza
dough (see page 34)
½ cup homemade pizza sauce
(see page 35)
1 cup grated mozzarella cheese
1 cup chopped marinated
porcini mushrooms
Extra virgin olive oil

DUST A SMOOTH working surface with flour. Place pizza dough ball in the center. Flatten the dough into a disc shape with your fingers. Next, roll the dough with a rolling pin until it is thin and reaches a diameter of 10 to 12 inches. Spoon the sauce evenly over the top and sprinkle with cheese and the mushrooms.

USING A METAL or wood peel, place the pizza in the wood-fired oven, away from the fire, and let bake several minutes. Turn the pizza 180 degrees and continue baking another few minutes or until crust is golden brown and the cheese is bubbly. Remove pizza from oven. Finish with a drizzle of olive oil.

NOTE: IF USING a conventional oven, cook pizza at 450 degrees F on a preheated pizza stone on the middle oven rack.

FIRESTONE
VINEYARD

FIRESTONE WINERY SYRAH, SANTA BARBARA

This wonderful Syrah offers deep black fruit aromas with hints of plum, blackberry, vanilla, and nutmeg. A full, juicy texture unfolds with flavors of blackberry and raspberry, while a subtle smoky quality adds complexity to the palate. Accents of mocha and white pepper accompany smooth, supple tannins on a long finish.

MEAT PIZZAS

For the carnivores of

the world, this chapter is for you. For those who may not be familiar with the names of some Italian meats, let's run down the list.

Bresaola is an air-cured salted beef that has aged for several months until the meat is hard and dark red or almost purple in color. The cut is lean and tender with a rather sweet smell. Bresaola comes from northern Italy, but can now be found in specialty shops throughout the U.S.

Calabrese salami is actually an Italian dry sausage made with pork (although sometimes a small amount of beef is added). The heat that gives this salami its kick is from adding hot peppers to the mixture, making this a very spicy and flavorful addition to any pizza.

Many of us have heard of prosciutto, but for those who have not, it is simply the Italian word for "ham." To make prosciutto, ham is salted and air-dried for up to two years. After curing, the prosciutto is sliced paper-thin, looking almost transparent. In this chapter, Chef Leonardo uses both traditional prosciutto and one made with duck breast. Assuming you have heard of quail and Italian sausage, the last two meats Chef Leonardo uses are speck and pancetta. Speck, like prosciutto, is a salt and air-cured ham, but cold-smoked with juniper berries and spices that give it a unique flavor. Pancetta is another word for Italian bacon, but comes from the belly of the pig and is cured with salt, pepper, and other spices, and is not smoked.

All of these wonderful Italian meats are available at Italian speciality shops, fine grocery stores, or on the Internet.

ARUGULA, BRESAOLA, AND PARMESAN CHEESE

MAKES 1 (10-INCH) PIZZA

1 (6- to 7-ounce) ball fresh pizza
dough (see page 34)
½ cup homemade pizza sauce
(see page 35)
1 cup grated mozzarella cheese
4 thin slices bresaola (Italian
salted beef)
1 cup fresh arugula
¼ cup shaved Parmesan cheese
Extra virgin olive oil

DUST A SMOOTH working surface with flour. Place pizza dough ball in the center. Flatten the dough into a disc shape with your fingers. Next, roll the dough with a rolling pin until it is thin and reaches a diameter of 10 to 12 inches. Spoon the sauce evenly over the top and sprinkle with the mozzarella cheese.

USING A METAL or wood peel, place the pizza in the wood-fired oven, away from the fire, and let bake several minutes. Turn the pizza 180 degrees and continue baking another few minutes or until crust is golden brown and the cheese is bubbly. Remove pizza from the oven. Add the bresaola, arugula, Parmesan cheese, and a drizzle of olive oil.

NOTE: IF USING a conventional oven, cook pizza at 450 degrees F on a preheated pizza stone on the middle oven rack.

MONTICELLO VINEYARDS

MONTICELLO VINEYARDS ESTATE-GROWN PINOT NOIR

This wine has very strong red-berry aromatics, including raspberry and strawberry. There are hints of ginger, clove, and vanilla, which accent the fruit. It is a medium- to full-bodied wine that has a very nice balance of fruit and acidity. Designed to be enjoyed young, this wine tastes great upon release and will continue to develop and drink well.

CALABRESE SALAMI

MAKES 1 (10-INCH) PIZZA

1 (6- to 7-ounce) ball fresh
pizza dough (see page 34)
½ cup homemade pizza
sauce (see page 35)
1 cup grated mozzarella cheese
10 to 12 slices Calabrese salami
½ tablespoon dried oregano
Extra virgin olive oil

DUST A SMOOTH working surface with flour. Place pizza dough ball in the center. Flatten the dough into a disc shape with your fingers. Next, roll the dough with a rolling pin until it is thin and reaches a diameter of 10 to 12 inches. Spoon the sauce evenly over the top and sprinkle with the cheese. Layer the salami on top, covering the entire pizza.

USING A METAL or wood peel, place the pizza in the wood-fired oven, away from the fire, and let bake several minutes. Turn the pizza 180 degrees and continue baking another few minutes or until crust is golden brown and the cheese is bubbly. Remove pizza from the oven. Sprinkle with the oregano and drizzle with olive oil.

NOTE: IF USING a conventional oven, cook pizza at 450 degrees F on a preheated pizza stone on the middle oven rack.

GREAT OAKS RANCH & VINEYARD
WINDMILL HILL CUVÉE

The Windmill Hill Cuvée is a delight to all senses. The wine's beautiful garnet color is highlighted with a vermillion edge and jewel-like glints of clarity. A swirl unleashes a bouquet of framboise, cassis, and toasty notes. A first sip and a silky-smooth texture emerges followed by mocha, cranberry, black plum, and hints of violets. The finish is stylish and lasting.

ITALIAN FIG AND PROSCIUTTO

MAKES 1 (10-INCH) PIZZA

1 (6- to 7-ounce) ball fresh pizza
dough (see page 34)
½ cup homemade pizza sauce
(see page 35)
1 cup grated mozzarella cheese
8 slices fresh Italian figs
4 to 6 slices prosciutto
6 to 8 fresh basil leaves
½ tablespoon dried oregano
Extra virgin olive oil

DUST A SMOOTH working surface with flour. Place pizza dough ball in the center. Flatten the dough into a disc shape with your fingers. Next, roll the dough with a rolling pin until it is thin and reaches a diameter of 10 to 12 inches. Spoon the sauce evenly over the top and sprinkle with the cheese. Arrange the fig slices on top.

USING A METAL or wood peel, place the pizza in the wood-fired oven, away from the fire, and let bake several minutes. Turn the pizza 180 degrees and continue baking another few minutes or until crust is golden brown and the cheese is bubbly. Remove pizza from the oven. Arrange the prosciutto on top. Sprinkle with basil leaves and oregano, and drizzle with olive oil.

NOTE: IF USING a conventional oven, cook pizza at 450 degrees F on a preheated pizza stone on the middle oven rack.

ARBIOS CELLARS
PRAXIS CENTRAL COAST LAGREIN

Pronounced Lah-GRAYHN, these grapes have been grown in Northern Italy for more than three hundred years. With an American Lagrein on California's Central Coast, Arbios introduces a medium-bodied wine with a silky mouthfeel. This Lagrein is deep, dark red, and has the body of a Merlot. Rich, ripe plum and berry flavors are accented by nuances of vanilla and chocolate.

DUCK PROSCIUTTO AND GORGONZOLA DOLCE

MAKES 1 (10-INCH) PIZZA

1 (6- to 7-ounce) ball fresh pizza dough (see page 34)
½ cup homemade pizza sauce (see page 35)
1 cup grated mozzarella cheese
6 to 8 dollops Gorgonzola cheese
8 slices duck prosciutto
6 to 8 fresh basil leaves
½ tablespoon dried oregano
Extra virgin olive oil

DUST A SMOOTH working surface with flour. Place pizza dough ball in the center. Flatten the dough into a disc shape with your fingers. Next, roll the dough with a rolling pin until it is thin and reaches a diameter of 10 to 12 inches. Spoon the sauce evenly over the top and sprinkle with the mozzarella cheese. Arrange the Gorgonzola cheese on top.

USING A METAL or wood peel, place the pizza in the wood-fired oven, away from the fire, and let bake several minutes. Turn the pizza 180 degrees and continue baking another few minutes or until crust is golden brown and the cheese is bubbly. Remove pizza from the oven. Arrange the prosciutto on top. Sprinkle with basil leaves and oregano and drizzle with olive oil.

NOTE: IF USING a conventional oven, cook pizza at 450 degrees F on a preheated pizza stone on the middle oven rack.

KOEHLER WINERY GRENACHE

Koehler Winery's 100 percent Grenache is grown and produced on the estate. The nose is bright and spicy offering Bing cherries and hints of pepper boldly accompanied by chocolate and blueberries on the palate with a long fruit–laden finish. This medium body Rhone-style varietal is a great wine to drink now or cellar for later.

BROCCOLI RABE AND SWEET ITALIAN SAUSAGE

MAKES 1 (10-INCH) PIZZA

1 (6- to 7-ounce) ball fresh pizza
dough (see page 34)
1 cup grated mozzarella cheese
10 to 12 slices grilled sweet
Italian sausage
2 cups fresh broccoli rabe or rapini
1 clove garlic, crushed
Extra virgin olive oil
½ tablespoon dried oregano

DUST A SMOOTH working surface with flour. Place pizza dough ball in the center. Flatten the dough into a disc shape with your fingers. Next, roll the dough with a rolling pin until it is thin and reaches a diameter of 10 to 12 inches. Sprinkle with the cheese; set aside.

TO PREPARE THE sausage, grill on an outdoor grill or roast in the pizza oven until well cooked in the center.

TO PREPARE THE broccoli rabe, remove the stalks before adding only the blossoms to a sauté pan over medium-high heat with the garlic and 2 tablespoons olive oil. Sauté until the broccoli rabe is wilted. Arrange the sausage and broccoli rabe on pizza.

USING A METAL or wood peel, place the pizza in the wood-fired oven, away from the fire, and let bake several minutes. Turn the pizza 180 degrees and continue baking another few minutes or until crust is golden brown and the cheese is bubbly. Remove pizza from the oven. Sprinkle with oregano and drizzle with olive oil.

NOTE: IF USING a conventional oven, cook pizza at 450 degrees F on a preheated pizza stone on the middle oven rack.

DRY CREEK VINEYARD HERITAGE ZINFANDEL

This wine begins with a deep and inky purple-red color. At first swirl, up front fruit aromas of wild blackberry and plum are evident along with subtle layers of white pepper and cardamom spice. On the palate, the flavors are rich and concentrated with additional blackberry characters that mingle with chocolate, allspice, and vanilla. This is an elegant, sophisticated, and polished Zinfandel.

CARAMELIZED ONION, ITALIAN SAUSAGE, AND ROASTED RED PEPPERS

MAKES 1 (10-INCH) PIZZA

1 (6- to 7-ounce) ball fresh pizza dough (see page 34)
½ cup homemade pizza sauce (see page 35)
1 cup grated mozzarella cheese
10 to 12 slices grilled sweet Italian sausage
½ cup sliced yellow onion
2 tablespoons butter
8 thin strips roasted red bell pepper (see page 70)
½ tablespoon dried oregano
Extra virgin olive oil

DUST A SMOOTH working surface with flour. Place pizza dough ball in the center. Flatten the dough into a disc shape with your fingers. Next, roll the dough with a rolling pin until it is thin and reaches a diameter of 10 to 12 inches. Spoon the sauce evenly over the top and sprinkle with the cheese; set aside.

TO PREPARE THE sausage, grill on an outdoor grill or roast in the pizza oven until well cooked in the center.

TO PREPARE THE caramelized onion, sauté onion slices in butter over medium-high heat until golden brown. Arrange the sausage, bell peppers, and caramelized onion on top of pizza.

USING A METAL or wood peel, place the pizza in the wood-fired oven, away from the fire, and let bake several minutes. Turn the pizza 180 degrees and continue baking another few minutes or until crust is golden brown and the cheese is bubbly. Remove pizza from the oven. Sprinkle with oregano and drizzle with olive oil.

NOTE: IF USING a conventional oven, cook pizza at 450 degrees F on a preheated pizza stone on the middle oven rack.

ROBERT HALL WINERY
RHONE DE ROBLES

The aroma of Robert Hall's Rhone de Robles is reminiscent of cherry and cranberry with hints of black pepper and spice. The color is deep ruby red and hints at the concentration of mouth-filling flavors that are the reward at tasting. This Rhone-style blend is a perfect food wine with fruit flavor delicately balanced by rich, silky tannins.

POACHED PEAR, GORGONZOLA, AND SPECK

MAKES 1 (10-INCH) PIZZA

1 (6- to 7-ounce) ball fresh pizza dough (see page 34)
1 cup grated mozzarella cheese
8 slices poached pear (canned or homemade)
6 to 8 dollops Gorgonzola cheese
4 to 6 slices Speck (juniper-flavored prosciutto)
1/2 tablespoon dried oregano
Extra virgin olive oil

DUST A SMOOTH working surface with flour. Place pizza dough ball in the center. Flatten the dough into a disc shape with your fingers. Next, roll the dough with a rolling pin until it is thin and reaches a diameter of 10 to 12 inches. Sprinkle with the mozzarella cheese. Arrange the pear slices and Gorgonzola cheese over top.

USING A METAL or wood peel, place the pizza in the wood-fired oven, away from the fire, and let bake several minutes. Turn the pizza 180 degrees and continue baking another few minutes or until crust is golden brown and the cheese is bubbly. Remove pizza from the oven. Arrange the slices of Speck on top. Sprinkle with oregano and drizzle with olive oil.

NOTE: IF USING a conventional oven, cook pizza at 450 degrees F on a preheated pizza stone on the middle oven rack.

EOS ESTATE
WINERY

EOS WINERY RESERVE CABERNET SAUVIGNON

The nose of this Cabernet is brimming with delightful aromas of chocolate, raspberries, and also some earthiness, the signature of East Side Paso Robles Reds. These aromas translate beautifully into flavors on the palate. Black cherries add to the richness of the mouthfeel as do nuances of smokiness in the lingering finish.

FRESH CHANTERELLE AND GRILLED QUAIL

MAKES 1 (10-INCH) PIZZA

1 (6- to 7-ounce) ball fresh pizza dough (see page 34)
1 cup grated mozzarella cheese
½ cup crème fraîche
6 to 8 thin slices fresh chanterelle mushrooms
8 slices grilled quail
½ tablespoon dried oregano
Extra virgin olive oil

DUST A SMOOTH working surface with flour. Place pizza dough ball in the center. Flatten the dough into a disc shape with your fingers. Next, roll the dough with a rolling pin until it is thin and reaches a diameter of 10 to 12 inches. Sprinkle with the cheese. Place dollops of crème fraîche, and the chanterelles and quail on top.

USING A METAL or wood peel, place the pizza in the wood-fired oven, away from the fire, and let bake several minutes. Turn the pizza 180 degrees and continue baking another few minutes or until crust is golden brown and the cheese is bubbly. Remove pizza from the oven. Sprinkle with oregano and drizzle with olive oil.

NOTE: IF USING a conventional oven, cook pizza at 450 degrees F on a preheated pizza stone on the middle oven rack.

MAURITSON FAMILY WINERY DRY ZINFANDEL

Vibrant aromas lie beneath the silky tannin and soft rich mouthfeel of this wine, which is made from fruit grown in the Rockpile appellation. With a very long and cool growing season, bright acidity gives this wine phenomenal balance.

PANCETTA AND WHITE ASPARAGUS

MAKES 1 (10-INCH) PIZZA

1 (6- to 7-ounce) ball fresh pizza dough (see page 34)
1/2 cup homemade pizza sauce (see page 35)
1 cup grated mozzarella cheese
4 to 6 fresh white asparagus stalks and tips, steamed and sliced diagonally (jarred variety is fine)
4 to 6 slices pancetta
1/2 tablespoon dried oregano
Extra virgin olive oil

DUST A SMOOTH working surface with flour. Place pizza dough ball in the center. Flatten the dough into a disc shape with your fingers. Next, roll the dough with a rolling pin until it is thin and reaches a diameter of 10 to 12 inches. Spoon the sauce evenly over the top and sprinkle with the cheese. Arrange the slices of asparagus and pancetta over top.

USING A METAL or wood peel, place the pizza in the wood-fired oven, away from the fire, and let bake several minutes. Turn the pizza 180 degrees and continue baking another few minutes or until crust is golden brown and the cheese is bubbly. Remove pizza from the oven. Sprinkle with oregano and drizzle with olive oil.

NOTE: IF USING a conventional oven, cook pizza at 450 degrees F on a preheated pizza stone on the middle oven rack.

CAMBRIA ESTATE WINERY JULIA'S VINEYARD PINOT NOIR

Julia's Vineyard is located on the cooler, western end of the Cambria Estate in Northern Santa Barbara County where the soils are ideal for Pinot Noir. Enjoy fresh cherry, blueberry, strawberry, and cranberry fruit flavors accented with cinnamon and vanilla oak spice characters. The mid-palate has a silky texture and balanced tannins that lead into a fruity and earthy finish.

SEAFOOD PIZZAS

With enthusiasm for

seafood at an all-time high and overnight airfreight shrinking our globe, we are facing an array of choices like never before. And that's a good thing, especially when it comes to selecting creative toppings for pizza.

Whether it's sinking your teeth into a hand-crafted pizza topped with shrimp and marinated porcini mushrooms, clams and tomato, or smoked Alaskan salmon, king crab, and lobster, seafood is the sure-fire way to please your guests, so long as the seafood is fresh.

When selecting seafood, find out which seafood you should purchase as a wild-caught variety, and which should be farm-raised. For the more ethically minded, learn the difference between seafood harvested in U.S.

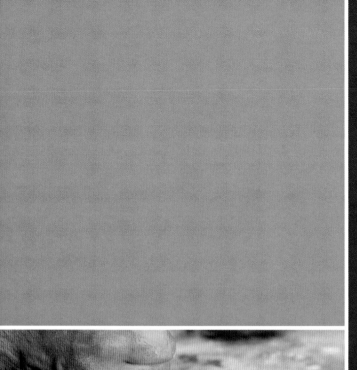

waters and those brought in from overseas. All these elements play a vital role in purchasing the best and freshest seafood available. To help educate yourself further, visit the Monterey Bay Aquarium's Seafood Watch Program—a leader in informing the public about the ever-changing seafood industry at: www.montereybayaquarium.org/cr/seafoodwatch.aspx.

For Chef Leonardo's mouthwatering seafood pizzas, appropriate seafood selections have been made for you. Feel free to experiment, try other fish, and see what you like best. Regardless of what you choose, always buy from a reliable source, and always buy fresh whenever possible.

One last note, not all of the seafood pizzas in this chapter contain homemade pizza sauce and mozzarella cheese. If you don't see one listed in the recipe, it is not that the chef forgot—it is simply not necessary!

SHRIMP WITH MARINATED PORCINI MUSHROOMS

MAKES 1 (10-INCH) PIZZA

1 (6- to 7-ounce) ball fresh pizza
dough (see page 34)
½ cup homemade pizza sauce
(see page 35)
1 cup grated mozzarella cheese
8 large shrimp, peeled, deveined,
and cooked (U.S. or Canada
caught Spot Prawn)
8 to 10 slices marinated porcini
mushrooms (jarred)
6 to 8 fresh basil leaves
½ tablespoon dried oregano
Extra virgin olive oil

DUST A SMOOTH working surface with flour. Place pizza dough ball in the center. Flatten the dough into a disc shape with your fingers. Next, roll the dough with a rolling pin until it is thin and reaches a diameter of 10 to 12 inches. Spoon the sauce evenly over the top and sprinkle with the cheese. Arrange the shrimp and mushrooms over top.

USING A METAL or wood peel, place the pizza in the wood-fired oven, away from the fire, and let bake several minutes. Turn the pizza 180 degrees and continue baking another few minutes or until crust is golden brown and the cheese is bubbly. Remove pizza from the oven. Sprinkle with basil leaves and oregano and drizzle with olive oil.

NOTE: IF USING a conventional oven, cook pizza at 450 degrees F on a preheated pizza stone on the middle oven rack.

BYRON

BYRON WINERY
BIEN NACIDO VINEYARD PINOT NOIR

This beautiful balanced wine displays aromas of red cherry, cedar, cardamom, and tobacco with undertones of earth and smokiness. On the palate, the wine offers excellent intensity of flavors, featuring Bing cherry, cranberry, and brown spice with hints of sandalwood and subtle French oak. The wine culminates in a long, smoky finish.

MANILA CLAMS WITH TOMATO

MAKES 1 (10-INCH) PIZZA

1 (6- to 7-ounce) ball fresh pizza
dough (see page 34)
½ cup homemade pizza sauce
(see page 35)
2 pounds live manila clams (farmed
or wild-caught steamers)
2 to 3 cloves garlic, crushed
Sea salt and black pepper to taste
1 cup white wine
6 to 8 fresh basil leaves
½ tablespoon dried oregano
Extra virgin olive oil

DUST A SMOOTH working surface with flour. Place pizza dough ball in the center. Flatten the dough into a disc shape with your fingers. Next, roll the dough with a rolling pin until it is thin and reaches a diameter of 10 to 12 inches. Spoon the sauce evenly over the top; set aside.

TO PREPARE THE clams, bring the garlic, salt, pepper, and wine to a boil. Add the clams and sauté until they open. Remove from heat, drain, and let cool. Discard any unopen clams. Remove the meat from the shells, reserving 4 or 5 clams in their shells. Arrange the clams on top of the pizza, including those reserved in their shells for presentation.

USING A METAL or wood peel, place the pizza in the wood-fired oven, away from the fire, and let bake several minutes. Turn the pizza 180 degrees and continue baking another few minutes or until crust is golden brown. Remove pizza from the oven. Sprinkle with basil leaves and oregano and drizzle with olive oil.

NOTE: IF USING a conventional oven, cook pizza at 450 degrees F on a preheated pizza stone on the middle oven rack.

**KINTON WINES
SYRAH**

Kinton is dedicated to producing Syrah from some of the finest vineyard sites in Santa Barbara County. Their wines are dense and concentrated, elegant and sleek. Enjoy this racy varietal with plum and dark berry, brightened by high notes of cherry, spiced with black pepper, and scented in the essence of smoky dark chocolate.

ALASKAN KING CRAB WITH CORN AND CHIVES

MAKES 1 (10-INCH) PIZZA

1 (6- to 7-ounce) ball fresh pizza dough (see page 34)
½ cup diced fresh tomato
1 cup grated mozzarella cheese
¼ cup crème fraîche
1 to 2 Alaskan king crab legs (U.S. wild-caught)
1 fresh yellow corn on the cob, in husk
6 to 8 fresh basil leaves
Handful of fresh chives, chopped
½ tablespoon dried oregano
Extra virgin olive oil

DUST A SMOOTH working surface with flour. Place pizza dough ball in the center. Flatten and round out the dough with your fingers. Next, roll the dough with a rolling pin until it is thin and reaches a diameter of 10 to 12 inches. Spoon the tomato evenly over the top and sprinkle with the cheese. Arrange dollops of crème fraîche and pieces of king crab on top; set aside.

TO PREPARE THE corn, soak the husk in water for about 30 minutes, then grill using an outdoor grill or wood-fired oven for about 10 minutes. Remove from heat and let cool. With a knife, strip the kernels off the cob and add to pizza.

USING A METAL or wood peel, place the pizza in the wood-fired oven, away from the fire, and let bake several minutes. Turn the pizza 180 degrees and continue baking another few minutes or until crust is golden brown. Remove pizza from oven. Sprinkle with basil leaves, chives, and oregano, and drizzle with olive oil.

NOTE: IF USING a conventional oven, cook pizza at 450 degrees F on a preheated pizza stone on the middle oven rack.

IO WINES SYRAH, UPPER BENCH

Io's Syrah Upper Bench bears the name of princess Io from Greek mythology, and is an excellent illustration of the complexity, spice, and full, lush tannins that result from the Upper Bench vineyards. The wine is well structured with aromas of white and black pepper, leather, and smoke. The flavors are concentrated with hints of blackberry, blueberry, spice, and a tasty, smoky finish. The texture is richly layered with firm tannins and a lingering fruit finish.

CALAMARI, MANILA CLAMS, MUSSELS, AND SHRIMP WITH FRESH GARLIC AND OREGANO

MAKES 1 (10-INCH) PIZZA

1 (6- to 7-ounce) ball fresh pizza dough (see page 34)
½ cup homemade pizza sauce (see page 35)
1 cup grated mozzarella cheese
3 cloves garlic, crushed, divided
Sea salt and black pepper to taste
2 cups white wine
¼ pound fresh calamari, cleaned (U.S. wild-caught)
½ pound fresh manila clams (farmed or wild-caught steamers)
½ pound fresh mussels (farmed)
¼ pound fresh uncooked shrimp, peeled and deveined (Pink shrimp; U.S wild-caught or farmed)
½ tablespoon chopped fresh oregano
Extra virgin olive oil

DUST A SMOOTH working surface with flour. Place pizza dough ball in the center. Flatten the dough into a disc shape with your fingers. Next, roll the dough with a rolling pin until it is thin and reaches a diameter of 10 to 12 inches. Spoon the sauce evenly over the top and sprinkle with the cheese; set aside.

TO PREPARE THE seafood, bring 2 cloves crushed garlic, salt, pepper, and wine to a boil. Add the calamari, clams, mussels, and shrimp and sauté until the calamari and shrimp are tender, and the clams and mussels have opened. Remove from heat, drain, and let cool. Discard any unopen clams or mussels. Remove the meat from the shells, reserving 4 or 5 clams and mussels in their shells. Divide the sautéed seafood on the pizza in four sections, keeping some of the clams and mussels in their shells for presentation. Sprinkle remaining garlic on top.

USING A METAL or wood peel, place the pizza in the wood-fired oven, away from the fire, and let bake several minutes. Turn the pizza 180 degrees and continue baking another few minutes or until crust is golden brown and the cheese is bubbly. Remove pizza from the oven. Sprinkle with oregano and drizzle with olive oil.

NOTE: IF USING a conventional oven, cook pizza at 450 degrees F on a preheated pizza stone on the middle oven rack.

TABLAS CREEK VINEYARD VERMENTINO

Tablas Creek is known for bottling this traditional Mediterranean varietal, found principally in Sardinia, Corsica, and Northern Italy, from its certified organic estate vineyard in Paso Robles. The Vermentino grape produces a wine that is bright, clean, and crisp, with distinctive citrus character, refreshing acidity, and surprising richness.

SMOKED SALMON WITH FRESH MASCARPONE, CAVIAR, CHIVES, RED ONION, AND CAPERS

MAKES 1 (10-INCH) PIZZA

1 (6- to 7-ounce) ball fresh pizza dough (see page 34)
½ cup homemade pizza sauce (see page 35)
1 cup grated mozzarella cheese
4 tablespoons fresh mascarpone cheese
1 cup fresh Alaskan smoked salmon, broken into pieces (U.S. wild-caught)
¼ cup sliced red onion
4 teaspoons fresh high-quality caviar (U.S. farmed sturgeon)
Handful of fresh chives
2 tablespoons capers
Extra virgin olive oil

DUST A SMOOTH working surface with flour. Place pizza dough ball in the center. Flatten the dough into a disc shape with your fingers. Next, roll the dough with a rolling pin until it is thin and reaches a diameter of 10 to 12 inches. Spoon the sauce evenly over the top and sprinkle with the mozzarella cheese.

USING A METAL or wood peel, place the pizza in the wood-fired oven, away from the fire, and let bake several minutes. Turn the pizza 180 degrees and continue baking another few minutes or until crust is golden brown and the cheese is bubbly. Remove pizza from the oven. Add dollops of mascarpone cheese, and arrange the salmon, onion, and caviar on top. Sprinkle with chives and capers and drizzle with olive oil.

NOTE: IF USING a conventional oven, cook pizza at 450 degrees F on a preheated pizza stone on the middle oven rack.

BUTTONWOOD FARM WINERY DEVIN (WHITE BORDEAUX-STYLE BLEND)

Buttonwood's Devin blends substantial portions of a sassy Sauvignon Blanc with light touches of oak and butter with a rich Semillon. The result is a wonderful gooseberry and ruby grapefruit flavor that melts into a slightly toasted finish adding dimension and warmth to the lively fruit flavors.

LOBSTER WITH RIPE AVOCADO AND SLICED TOMATO

MAKES 1 (10-INCH) PIZZA

1 (6- to 7-ounce) ball fresh pizza dough (see page 34)
1 cup grated mozzarella cheese
¼ cup crème fraîche
1 live Maine or spiny lobster, cooked (U.S. or Baja trap-caught)
1 ripe avocado, pitted, peeled, and sliced
1 cup sliced fresh cherry tomatoes
Handful of fresh arugula leaves
Extra virgin olive oil

DUST A SMOOTH working surface with flour. Place pizza dough ball in the center. Flatten and round out the dough with your fingers. Next, roll the dough with a rolling pin until it is thin and reaches a diameter of 10 to 12 inches. Sprinkle generously with the mozzarella cheese, and then add 4 dollops of crème fraîche; set aside.

TO PREPARE THE lobster, submerge live lobster in a pot of boiling salted water. Cook about 10 minutes once the water returns to a boil, until the shell is bright red. Remove lobster and let cool. Remove tail meat and slice into medallions. Arrange the sliced lobster medallions on top of pizza. (NOTE: If using Main lobster, remove and slice claw meat, and place on top of pizza too.)

USING A METAL or wood peel, place the pizza in the wood-fired oven, away from the fire, and let bake several minutes. Turn the pizza 180 degrees and continue baking another few minutes or until crust is golden brown. Remove pizza from oven. Arrange the avocado and tomatoes on top, along with the arugula. Finish with a drizzle of olive oil.

NOTE: IF USING a conventional oven, cook pizza at 450 degrees F on a preheated pizza stone on the middle oven rack.

CASTORO CELLARS
ESTATE VIOGNIER STONE'S THROW

This Estate Viognier is entirely from Castoro Cellars Stone's Throw Vineyard. A cold fermentation in stainless steel tanks retains the inherently floral varietal aromas. After fermentation, the wine is transferred to American oak barrels for almost four months to add complexity. This Viognier is dry and crisp with high flavor intensity.

MUSSELS WITH BLACK PEPPER, GARLIC, AND OLIVE OIL

MAKES 1 (10-INCH) PIZZA

1 (6- to 7-ounce) ball fresh pizza dough (see page 34)
½ cup homemade pizza sauce (see page 35)
2 pounds fresh mussels (farmed)
3 cloves garlic, crushed, divided
Sea salt to taste
1 cup white wine
Coarse black pepper to taste
Extra virgin olive oil

DUST A SMOOTH working surface with flour. Place pizza dough ball in the center. Flatten the dough into a disc shape with your fingers. Next, roll the dough with a rolling pin until it is thin and reaches a diameter of 10 to 12 inches. Spoon the sauce evenly over the top; set aside.

TO PREPARE THE mussels, bring 2 cloves crushed garlic, salt, and wine to a boil. Add the mussels and sauté until the shells have opened. Remove from heat, drain, and let cool. Discard any unopen shells. Remove the meat from the shells, reserving 4 or 5 mussels in their shells. Arrange the mussels on the pizza, keeping 4 or 5 in their shells for presentation. Sprinkle remaining garlic and pepper on top.

USING A METAL or wood peel, place the pizza in the wood-fired oven, away from the fire, and let bake several minutes. Turn the pizza 180 degrees and continue baking another few minutes or until crust is golden brown. Remove pizza from the oven. Finish with a drizzle of olive oil.

NOTE: IF USING a conventional oven, cook pizza at 450 degrees F on a preheated pizza stone on the middle oven rack.

SUNSTONE WINERY PINOT GRIGIO

Sunstone's Pinot Grigio is light straw in color. Dry and light, with a slight crisp tanginess that everyone loves about this grape. That's just the beginning, though. The wine soon shows off its exotic side as amazing flavors of dried pear and subtle hints of guava envelop the palate, along with notes of pineapple, vanilla, and nutmeg. An enjoyable pairing with fresh seafood, summer salads, fruit, and cheese.

CALZONES, PANZEROTTIS, & SCHIACCIATAS

With leftover pizza sauce in the pot and extra pizza dough on the counter, now is the best time to try some other traditional Italian dishes. A popular choice is the calzone, basically a large turnover made from pizza dough and stuffed with cheese and other tasty ingredients. Chef Leonardo likes to finish his calzones by serving them topped with warm pizza sauce and a little on the side for dipping. A panzerotti is a baked or deep-fried calzone, but smaller than a typical calzone. Panzerottis are about the size of a Hostess fruit pie. The most important rule to remember when making a panzerotti is not to poke any holes on top of the dough like you would typically do with a calzone so steam can escape. Poking holes in panzerotti will make it quickly deflate

or fill with oil as soon as you begin to deep-fry. Make your panzerotti air- and oil-tight, and you will have yourself a wonderfully warm and crunchy treat. As for the schiacciata, think of it as a gently crushed or flattened calzone. Chef Leonardo prepares his schiacciatas by not sealing the edges like you would typically do with a calzone or panzerotti. He leaves the edges open, and using his fingers, gently presses down on top of the schiacciata to remove the air while molding the dough around the savory ingredients inside.

Three delicious and authentic dishes you can make with leftover pizza sauce and dough.

BROCCOLI, GRILLED EGGPLANT, MUSHROOM, ROASTED PEPPERS, AND WHITE TRUFFLE CALZONE

MAKES 1 CALZONE

1 (6- to 7-ounce) ball fresh pizza dough (see page 34)
1 cup grated mozzarella cheese
2 slices fresh eggplant
Extra virgin olive oil
Salt and pepper to taste
3 or 4 pieces fresh broccoli tops
¼ cup sliced fresh champion mushrooms
½ roasted red bell pepper (see page 70)
½ roasted yellow bell pepper (see page 70)
White truffle oil
Sea salt
Parmesan cheese, grated

DUST A SMOOTH working surface with flour. Place pizza dough ball in the center. Flatten and round out the dough with your fingers. Next, roll the dough with a rolling pin until it reaches a diameter of 8 to 10 inches. Sprinkle the mozzarella cheese over one half of the dough; set aside.

TO PREPARE THE eggplant, toss eggplant slices in a small bowl with a drizzle of olive oil and a pinch of salt and pepper, to coat. Transfer the eggplant to an outdoor grill, or inside the wood-fired oven, and cook until tender. Add eggplant along with the broccoli, mushrooms, and roasted bell peppers on top of the cheese on the calzone. Next, fold over the dough to seal in the ingredients, and press the edges of the dough together with your fingers. With a fork, make a few small holes on top so steam can escape.

USING A METAL or wood peel, place the calzone in the wood-fired oven, away from the fire, and let bake several minutes. Turn the calzone 180 degrees and continue baking another few minutes or until crust is golden brown. Remove calzone from oven. Drizzle the top with white truffle oil and sprinkle with sea salt and Parmesan cheese.

NOTE: IF USING a conventional oven, cook calzone at 450 degrees F on a preheated pizza stone on the middle oven rack.

DOG HILL VINEYARD SANGIOVETO RESERVE

Sangioveto Reserve is a traditional handmade wine. The grapes used by Dog Hill Vineyard are from very old head-pruned vines—some of the oldest in California. Aged in a variety of small oak barrels for a long lengthy rest, the wine showcases a nice balance of fruit with layers of black cherry and vanilla followed by a long complex finish.

BASIL, PARMESAN, AND PROSCIUTTO CALZONE

MAKES 1 CALZONE

1 (6- to 7-ounce) ball fresh pizza dough (see page 34)
1 cup grated mozzarella cheese
2 to 3 thin slices prosciutto
1 tablespoon grated Parmesan cheese
4 to 5 fresh basil leaves
Extra virgin olive oil
Sea salt
½ cup homemade pizza sauce (see page 35), warmed

DUST A SMOOTH working surface with flour. Place pizza dough ball in the center. Flatten and round out the dough with your fingers. Next, roll the dough with a rolling pin until it reaches a diameter of 8 to 10 inches. Sprinkle the mozzarella cheese over one half of the dough. On top of the cheese, add the prosciutto, Parmesan cheese, and basil leaves. Fold over the dough to seal in the ingredients, and press the edges of the dough together with your fingers. With a fork, make a few small holes on top so steam can escape.

USING A METAL or wood peel, place the calzone in the wood-fired oven, away from the fire, and let bake several minutes. Turn the calzone 180 degrees and continue baking another few minutes or until crust is golden brown. Remove calzone from oven. Drizzle with olive oil and sprinkle with sea salt. Finish with warm pizza sauce over the top, reserving some on the side for dipping.

NOTE: IF USING a conventional oven, cook calzone at 450 degrees F on a preheated pizza stone on the middle oven rack.

PALMINA WINES DOLCETTO

Dolcetto is an easy-going, table-friendly wine. Dolcetto, whose name translates as "little sweet one," is a wine full of youthful exuberance, but also a wine with structure and balance. Enjoy a dark ruby color with amethyst highlights, which, with a swirl, produces aromas of raspberry and cherry, a bit of toast, and a hint of violets. Enjoy Dolcetto as in Italy—*da pronto bevere*—a wine to drink now.

TUSCAN SALAMI CALZONE

MAKES 1 CALZONE

1 (6- to 7-ounce) ball fresh pizza dough (see page 34)
1 cup grated mozzarella cheese
4 or 5 thin slices Italian salami
1 tablespoon grated Parmesan cheese
Extra virgin olive oil
Sea salt
½ cup homemade pizza sauce (see page 35), warmed

DUST A SMOOTH working surface with flour. Place pizza dough ball in the center. Flatten and round out the dough with your fingers. Next, roll the dough with a rolling pin until it reaches a diameter of 8 to 10 inches. Sprinkle the mozzarella cheese over one half of the dough. On top of the cheese, add the salami and Parmesan cheese. Fold over the dough to seal in the ingredients, and press the edges of the dough together with your fingers. With a fork, make a few small holes on top so steam can escape.

USING A METAL or wood peel, place the calzone in the wood-fired oven, away from the fire, and let bake for several minutes. Turn the calzone 180 degrees and continue baking for another few minutes or until crust is golden brown. Remove calzone from oven. Drizzle with olive oil and sprinkle with sea salt. Finish with warm pizza sauce over the top, reserving some on the side for dipping.

NOTE: IF USING a conventional oven, cook calzone at 450 degrees F on a preheated pizza stone on the middle oven rack.

GAINEY VINEYARD
LIMITED SELECTION SYRAH

While this Syrah is delicious on its own, the pleasure will be magnified by pairing it with the Tuscan Salami Calzone. In the nose, experience warm, inviting aromas of lavish black fruits with unmistakable scents of white pepper, licorice, brown spices, cocoa, and toasty oak. On the dense, concentrated palate, sumptuous blackberry and black raspberry flavors gain structure and depth from ripe, seamlessly integrated tannins. A long, plush and savory finish completes the experience.

RICOTTA CALZONE

MAKES 1 CALZONE

1 (6- to 7-ounce) ball fresh pizza
dough (see page 34)
1 cup ricotta cheese
1 tablespoon grated Parmesan
cheese
4 to 5 fresh basil leaves
Extra virgin olive oil
Sea salt
½ cup homemade pizza sauce
(see page 35), warmed

DUST A SMOOTH working surface with flour. Place pizza dough ball in the center. Flatten and round out the dough with your fingers. Next, roll the dough with a rolling pin until it reaches a diameter of 8 to 10 inches. Add the ricotta cheese to one half of the dough. Add the Parmesan cheese and basil leaves on top. Fold over the dough to seal in the ingredients, and press the edges of the dough together with your fingers. With a fork, make a few small holes on top so steam can escape.

USING A METAL or wood peel, place the calzone in the wood-fired oven, away from the fire, and let bake several minutes. Turn the calzone 180 degrees and continue baking another few minutes or until crust is golden brown. Remove calzone from oven. Drizzle with oil and sprinkle with sea salt. Finish with warm pizza sauce over the top, reserving some on the side for dipping.

NOTE: IF USING a conventional oven, cook calzone at 450 degrees F on a preheated pizza stone on the middle oven rack.

LINCOURT

LINCOURT VINEYARD CHARDONNAY, SANTA BARBARA COUNTY

The bright acidity and fresh fruit flavors render this Chardonnay a thoroughly quenching antidote for those suffering from palate fatigue. As in years past, this wine is sourced from Santa Maria's Bien Nacido Vineyard in combination with cool-climate fruit from vineyards in the Santa Rita Hills. The juicy tropical aromatics of coconut, mango, and papaya, and lush texture are the hallmarks of Bien Nacido, while Santa Rita Hills fruit lends more citric notes of mandarin orange and key lime.

PANZEROTTI WITH ANCHOVY, MOZZARELLA, AND TOMATO

MAKES 1 PANZEROTTI

1 (3- to 4-ounce) ball fresh pizza dough (see page 34)*

½ cup grated mozzarella cheese

1 tablespoon chopped hand-packed anchovy fillets, drained

1 fresh Roma tomato, chopped

Canola oil for deep-frying

Sea salt

¼ cup homemade pizza sauce (see page 35), warmed

DUST A SMOOTH working surface with flour. Place pizza dough ball in the center. Flatten and round out the dough with your fingers. Next, roll the dough with a rolling pin until it reaches a diameter of 4 to 5 inches. Add the cheese to one half of the dough. Add the anchovy and tomato on top. Fold over the dough to seal in the ingredients, and press the edges of the dough together with your fingers. Do not make any air holes on top.

USING A SLOTTED spoon, gently place the panzerotti in a deep-fryer filled with canola oil. Fry for several minutes, or until crust is golden brown. Remove panzerotti from the fryer and drain on paper towels. Finish with a sprinkle of sea salt and serve with warm pizza sauce on the side for dipping.

*PANZEROTTIS ARE SMALL so only half the dough you would normally use for pizzas, calzones, or schiacciatas is used.

ARTISTE IMPRESSIONIST WINERY & TASTING STUDIO BUENA VIDA

This wine is a blend of 60% Tempranillo, 35% Syrah, and 5% Merlot. Floral and full of spiced-fruit aromatics, Buena Vida showcases Tempranillo's unique characteristics that only arise after it ages in oak. Sweet vanilla and hints of toffee abound, while thick undercurrents of plum and strawberry aromas course throughout. Delicate notes of rose petals swirl above it all.

PANZEROTTI WITH MOZZARELLA AND PROSCIUTTO

MAKES 1 PANZEROTTI

1 (3- to 4-ounce) ball fresh pizza dough (see page 34)*
½ cup grated mozzarella cheese
½ tablespoon grated Parmesan cheese
2 thin slices prosciutto
Canola oil for deep-frying
Sea salt
¼ cup homemade pizza sauce (see page 35), warmed

DUST A SMOOTH working surface with flour. Place pizza dough ball in the center. Flatten and round out the dough with your fingers. Next, roll the dough with a rolling pin until it reaches a diameter of 4 to 5 inches. Add the mozzarella cheese to one half of the dough. Add the Parmesan cheese and prosciutto on top. Fold over the dough to seal in the ingredients, and press the edges of the dough together with your fingers. Do not make any air holes on top.

USING A SLOTTED spoon, gently place the panzerotti in a deep-fryer filled with canola oil. Fry several minutes, or until crust is golden brown. Remove panzerotti from the fryer and drain on paper towels. Finish with a sprinkle of sea salt and serve with warm pizza sauce on the side for dipping.

*PANZEROTTIS ARE SMALL so only half the dough you would normally use for pizzas, calzones, or schiacciatas is used.

FOLEY VINEYARD PINOT NOIR, SANTA RITA HILLS

Foley

The Santa Rita Hills is a sub-appellation of the Santa Ynez Valley, an east–west valley that opens directly to the Pacific Ocean. This marine-influenced fruit offers an intense dark garnet color, rich flavor, and a bouquet that exudes aromas of blackberry, black cherry, raspberry, and boysenberry with hints of vanilla and baking spices.

SCHIACCIATA WITH BURRATA, ARUGULA, AND SPECK

MAKES 1 SCHIACCIATA

1 (6- to 7-ounce) ball fresh pizza dough (see page 34)

1 cup fresh Burrata cheese, broken into pieces

1 tablespoon grated Parmesan cheese

2 to 3 thin slices Speck (juniper-flavored prosciutto)

½ cup fresh arugula

Extra virgin olive oil

Sea salt

DUST A SMOOTH working surface with flour. Place pizza dough ball in the center. Flatten and round out the dough with your fingers. Next, roll the dough with a rolling pin until it reaches a diameter of 8 to 10 inches. Add the Burrata cheese to one half of the dough. Add the Parmesan cheese, Speck, and arugula on top. Fold over the dough to seal in the ingredients, but do not press the edges of the dough together like you would when making a calzone or panzerotti. Instead, softly poke your fingers over the top of the dough while pressing down. This will remove any air pockets while forming the dough around the ingredients.

USING A METAL or wood peel, place the schiacciata in the wood-fired oven, away from the fire, and let bake several minutes. Turn the schiacciata 180 degrees and continue baking another few minutes or until crust is golden brown. Remove schiacciata from oven. Drizzle with olive oil and sprinkle with sea salt. With a pizza cutter, slice into wedges and serve.

NOTE: IF USING a conventional oven, cook schiacciata at 450 degrees F on a pre-heated pizza stone on the middle oven rack.

CARHARTT VINEYARD SANGIOVESE, FAITH VINEYARD, SANTA YNEZ VALLEY

Carhartt's Sangiovese from their Faith Vineyard is an easy-to-drink wine with lovely spice undertones and bright red fruit, both on the nose and in the mouth. Enjoy this handcrafted Sangiovese with pizza, calzones, schiacciatas, and light pasta dishes.

SCHIACCIATA WITH COTTO SALAMI, MUSHROOM, AND PROSCIUTTO

MAKES 1 SCHIACCIATA

1 (6- to 7-ounce) ball fresh pizza dough (see page 34)
1 cup grated mozzarella cheese
1 tablespoon grated Parmesan cheese
2 to 3 thin slices cotto salami
½ cup sliced champion mushrooms
2 thin slices prosciutto
4 to 5 fresh basil leaves
Extra virgin olive oil
Sea salt

DUST A SMOOTH working surface with flour. Place pizza dough ball in the center. Flatten and round out the dough with your fingers. Next, roll the dough with a rolling pin until it reaches a diameter of 8 to 10 inches. Add the mozzarella cheese to one half of the dough. Add the Parmesan cheese, salami, mushrooms, prosciutto, and basil on top. Fold over the dough to seal in the ingredients, but do not press the edges of the dough together like you would when making a calzone or panzerotti. Instead, softly poke your fingers over the top of the dough while pressing down. This will remove any air pockets while forming the dough around the ingredients.

USING A METAL or wood peel, place the schiacciata in the wood-fired oven, away from the fire, and let bake several minutes. Turn the schiacciata 180 degrees and continue baking another few minutes or until crust is golden brown. Remove schiacciata from oven. Drizzle with olive oil and sprinkle with sea salt. With a pizza cutter, slice into wedges and serve.

NOTE: IF USING a conventional oven, cook schiacciata at 450 degrees F on a preheated pizza stone on the middle oven rack.

TRATTORIA GRAPPOLO PRIVATE LABEL GRAPPOLAIA, SANTA BARBARA COUNTY

Produced and bottled by Arthur Earl Winery in the Santa Ynez Valley, Grappolaia is a Super-Tuscan wine with Sangiovese and Bordeaux varieties. This combination has been producing some of the most popular and expensive wines from Italy for more than a decade. This restaurant version blends Merlot and Cabernet with Sangiovese to produce a delightful wine that is California in origin but truly Italian in spirit.

SCHIACCIATA WITH BRESAOLA AND PARMESAN

MAKES 1 SCHIACCIATA

1 (6- to 7-ounce) ball fresh pizza dough (see page 34)
1 cup grated mozzarella cheese
1 tablespoon grated Parmesan cheese
2 to 3 thin slices bresaola
4 to 5 fresh basil leaves
Extra virgin olive oil
Sea salt

DUST A SMOOTH working surface with flour. Place pizza dough ball in the center. Flatten and round out the dough with your fingers. Next, roll the dough with a rolling pin until it reaches a diameter of 8 to 10 inches. Add the mozzarella cheese to one half of the dough. Add the Parmesan cheese, bresaola, and basil leaves on top. Fold over the dough to seal in the ingredients, but do not press the edges of the dough together like you would when making a calzone or panzerotti. Instead, softly poke your fingers over the top of the dough while pressing down. This will remove any air pockets while forming the dough around the ingredients.

USING A METAL or wood peel, place the schiacciata in the wood-fired oven, away from the fire, and let bake several minutes. Turn the schiacciata 180 degrees and continue baking another few minutes or until crust is golden brown. Remove schiacciata from oven. Drizzle with olive oil and sprinkle with sea salt. With a pizza cutter, slice into wedges and serve.

NOTE: IF USING a conventional oven, cook schiacciata at 450 degrees F on a pre-heated pizza stone on the middle oven rack.

TRATTORIA GRAPPOLO PRIVATE LABEL SYRAH, SANTA BARBARA COUNTY

Produced and bottled by William James Cellars in Santa Ynez Valley, the restaurant's Private Label Syrah is aged in one-third new oak barrels. The wine has a rich, superior color, velvety mouthfeel, and is very easy drinking with ripe fruit aromas and flavors.

DELICIOUS DESSERTS

Like any typical dinner,

the homemade pizza experience is not complete without dessert. In this chapter, fresh fruits and nuts are the focal point of these light and surprisingly flavorful and original desserts.

The *Strawberry and Mascarpone Pizza* is sweet, luscious, and the perfect ending to an exciting pizza party. The *Pumpkin Pancakes* are fluffy, zesty, and burst with vivid memories of family gatherings. So too are the desserts made with fresh lemons. Whether it's a *Limoncello Cake* made with Italy's signature drink—a thick, icy cold iridescent yellow liqueur known as limoncello—or a decadent lemon cream tart, one taste of either and you will be dreaming of the lemon trees planted along Italy's

sunny coastline of Campania where floral and citrus aromas mingle with the fresh, salty tang of sea breezes.

Other hand-crafted favorites are Chef Leonardo's *Chestnut Pudding*, an *Almond Tart*, bread pudding made with light, buttery croissants, a colorful strawberry cocktail, and his signature *Zuccotto*—a marvelous combination of sponge cake, cognac, rum, and toasted hazelnuts filled with chocolate and whipped cream.

No matter what dessert you select, all of these extraordinary treats will be well received. They also pair well with a fresh roasted cup of Italian coffee, espresso, or finely-aged port.

STRAWBERRY AND MASCARPONE PIZZA

MAKES 1 (10-INCH) PIZZA

1 (6- to 7-ounce) ball fresh pizza dough (see page 34)
1 cup grated mozzarella cheese
4 tablespoons fresh mascarpone cheese
4 to 5 fresh strawberries, sliced

DUST A SMOOTH working surface with flour. Place pizza dough ball in the center. Flatten the dough into a disc shape with your fingers. Next, roll the dough with a rolling pin until it is thin and reaches a diameter of 10 to 12 inches. Sprinkle with the mozzarella cheese, and then dollop the mascarpone cheese on top.

USING A METAL or wood peel, place the pizza in the wood-fired oven, away from the fire, and let bake several minutes. Turn the pizza 180 degrees and continue baking another few minutes or until crust is golden brown. Remove pizza from oven. Arrange the strawberry slices evenly on top.

NOTE: IF USING a conventional oven, cook pizza at 450 degrees F on a preheated pizza stone on the middle oven rack.

PUMPKIN PANCAKES

SERVES 4

1 cup water
Zest of 1 lemon
2¼ cups fresh pumpkin, diced
3½ tablespoons sugar
½ cup golden raisins (pre-soaked
in water until soft)
1 teaspoon baking soda
Zest of 2 oranges
1 cup flour
Canola oil, for frying
Powdered sugar, for garnish

IN A SMALL saucepan over medium-high heat, add the water, lemon zest, and diced pumpkin until boiling. Lower heat and simmer while mashing pumpkin with a fork until a creamy texture is achieved. Remove from heat and let cool. Add the sugar, raisins, baking soda, orange zest, and flour; stir well and set aside.

IN A LARGE pan over medium-high heat, add the oil. When hot, ladle a large spoonful of the pumpkin mixture into the pan and fry 2 to 3 minutes, or until golden brown and crispy. Using a spatula, flip the cake over and cook the other side until crisp. Remove the cake and let drain on paper towels. Repeat the process until batter is gone.

TO SERVE, STACK several cakes on a serving plate and finish with a sprinkling of powdered sugar.

CARAMEL SAUCE

MAKES 1 QUART

4 cups sugar
4 cups water
2 cups heavy cream, room
temperature but not warm
1 teaspoon fresh lemon juice
1 cup whole milk
1 teaspoon vanilla extract
Pinch of salt

COMBINE THE SUGAR and water in a 2-quart saucepan. Stir to dissolve sugar only. Stop stirring and use a clean wet pastry brush to wash down any sugar crystals on the sides of the pan. Do this every few minutes. Turn heat on high and boil until a dark amber color is achieved. Slightly swirl the pan to even the cooking.

REDUCE HEAT TO low. Slowly add the cream while stirring. Remove from heat and add the lemon juice, milk, vanilla, and salt. Strain into a stainless container and stir periodically until cool. Cover with plastic wrap and refrigerate up to 1 week.

CRÈME CHANTILLY

MAKES 2 CUPS

2 cups heavy cream, chilled
2 tablespoons confectioners'
sugar, sifted
1 teaspoon vanilla extract

USING AN ELECTRIC mixer with a whisk attachment, whip cream until soft peaks form. Add sugar and vanilla and continue whipping until mixture starts to thicken. Remove contents and refrigerate until ready to use.

LEMON CREAM TART

SERVES 4 TO 6

TART CRUST
2⅔ cups flour
3 eggs
1 cup sugar
⅔ cup butter, softened
1 tablespoon vanilla extract
1½ tablespoons yeast

CREAM
3 large lemons, zested and juiced
½ cup flour
2 cups warm water
1 cup sugar
1 teaspoon vanilla extract
2 eggs
3½ tablespoons butter
1 tablespoon potato starch

TO MAKE THE crust, pour flour into a mountain and hollow out the center, leaving a little flour at the bottom. Add the eggs, sugar, butter, vanilla, and yeast. Mix well until a smooth dough ball has formed. Cover dough ball with a damp towel and let it sit in a cool place until double in size.

PREHEAT OVEN TO 350 degrees. Work dough lightly with hands then spread thinly with a rolling pin. Line tart pans with dough, reserving some for decoration. Fill with cream and cover with dough strips in a crisscross pattern. Bake until crust is golden brown.

TO MAKE THE cream, wash, zest, and peel the lemons, then squeeze and reserve juice. Place flour in a bowl and dissolve with warm water. Try to avoid lumps. Add sugar and vanilla. Beat eggs with a fork and add to mixture. Add lemon zest and juice, along with butter and starch. Pour mixture into a pan and heat over a low, stirring constantly until thick. Remove from heat and cover.

LIMONCELLO CAKE

SERVES 6 TO 8

1 (8½-inch) sponge cake
¼ cup quality vodka
2 to 3 cups whipped cream, divided
1 container fresh strawberries, sliced
½ cup limoncello liqueur
Candied lemon rinds and fresh lemon leaves

SPLIT THE SPONGE cake in half, lengthwise, and place the two rounds in a workable surface. Drizzle one half of the cake with the vodka (this will be the bottom layer). Spread 1 cup whipped cream over the soaked cake and top generously with slices of fresh strawberry. Place the other cake round on top of the strawberries and cream. Drizzle generously with the limoncello. Spread the remaining whipped cream to cover the entire cake.

DECORATE THE TOP with an arrangement of strawberries, candied lemon rinds, and lemon leaves, if desired.

ALMOND TART WITH RICOTTA

SERVES 8 TO 10

¾ cup ricotta
1 cup sugar, divided
1 stick butter, melted (½ cup)
5 eggs, separated
2 tablespoons brandy
1 cup flour
Pinch of salt
1 teaspoon baking powder
½ cup chopped almonds
Powdered sugar, for garnish

PREHEAT OVEN TO 175 degrees F.

IN A BOWL, combine the ricotta and ¹/₂ cup sugar. Add the melted butter and stir.

IN A SEPARATE bowl, combine the egg yolks, remaining sugar, and brandy. And the egg yolk mixture to the ricotta mixture and stir well. Add the flour, salt, baking powder, and almonds, and mix well; set aside.

IN A SMALL bowl, whisk the egg whites until stiff. Fold the egg whites into the egg yolk and ricotta mixture. Pour mixture into a greased 9-inch springform pan and bake for 40 to 45 minutes. Serve with powdered sugar on top.

STRAWBERRY COCKTAIL

SERVES 4

1½ cups water
1 cup sugar
Juice of 1 lemon
¼ cup white wine
2 containers fresh strawberries, large dice
¼ cup whipped cream
Ground cinnamon
Sprigs of fresh mint

IN A MEDIUM-SIZE bowl, add the water, sugar, lemon juice, and wine; mix well. Add the strawberries and let stand in the refrigerator for about 3 to 4 hours. To serve, divide the strawberries and juice into individual serving bowls. Top each bowl with a dollop of whipped cream, a dusting of cinnamon, and a fresh sprig of mint.

CHESTNUT PUDDING

SERVES 4

4 cups canned chestnuts, drained
2 cups whole milk
2 teaspoons vanilla extract
Pinch of salt
3½ tablespoons sugar
Zest from 1 orange
4 cups heavy whipping cream
4 teaspoons powdered sugar, for garnish
3½ tablespoons toasted chopped almonds

IN A SAUCEPAN over medium-low heat, add the chestnuts, milk, vanilla, and salt. Cover and simmer for about 15 minutes. Remove from heat and press through a potato ricer along with the liquid. (NOTE: A potato ricer is a kitchen utensil that processes food by forcing it through small holes. A ricer resembles a large garlic press and works in the same fashion.) Return the mashed contents to saucepan, add the sugar and orange zest. Turn heat to low and cook for about 5 minutes or until sugar is melted. Remove saucepan from heat and stir in the cream, mixing well. Pour the contents from saucepan into 4 ramekins and refrigerate for a least 3 hours. Just before serving, sprinkle with powdered sugar and top with the toasted almonds.

ZUCCOTTO

SERVES 4 TO 6

1 premade sponge cake
¼ cup rum
¼ cup cognac
2 cups whipped cream, divided
2 ounces toasted hazelnuts,
crumbled
2 ounces bittersweet
chocolate chips
Cocoa powder
Powdered sugar
Caramel Sauce (see page 152)

USING SMALL 3-INCH bowl-shaped molds (or something equivalent like a 3-inch glass bowl), line the inside with strips of sponge cake. Next, drizzle the cake generously with the rum and cognac. Using the back of a spoon, spread 1 cup of whipped cream over the moistened cake. Add the crumbled hazelnuts. Spread another layer of whipped cream, covering the hazelnuts, and add the chocolate chips. This should fill the inside of the cavity. With a sharp knife, trim off any excess cake hanging over the edge of the mold. Let stand in refrigerator 4 hours or overnight.

TO SERVE, FLIP each mold over onto a serving plate. Dust the top with cocoa powder, powdered sugar, and Caramel Sauce.

CROISSANT BREAD PUDDING WITH GOLDEN RAISINS, WHITE CHOCOLATE, AND CREAM SAUCE

SERVES 4

2 fresh croissants, cut and cubed

¼ cup Grand Marnier

4 tablespoons golden raisins

1½ cups milk

5 egg yolks

¼ cup sugar

1 teaspoon vanilla

4 tablespoons rum

English Cream Sauce (see below)

DIVIDE THE CROISSANT pieces into individual ramekins. Drizzle each ramekin generously with the Grand Marnier, and toss in the golden raisins.

PREHEAT THE OVEN to 375 degrees F. While oven is heating, mix the milk and egg yolks in a small bowl. Add the sugar and vanilla, and whisk until well combined. Pour the liquid evenly in each ramekin. Next, set the ramekins on a rimmed baking sheet and place in oven. Fill the bottom of the baking sheet with water so the pudding will bake evenly. Bake about 50 minutes, or until warm and golden-brown. Remove from oven and drizzle each ramekin with rum. Serve warm with the English Cream Sauce.

ENGLISH CREAM SAUCE

MAKES 2¼ CUPS

1 cup whole milk

1 cup heavy cream

½ cup sugar, divided

¼ vanilla bean, scraped into sugar

4 large egg yolks

½ teaspoon pure vanilla extract

IN A MEDIUM saucepan, bring milk, cream, $1/4$ cup sugar, and vanilla bean to a boil. In a small bowl, whisk together egg yolks and remaining sugar. Temper eggs by whisking in some of the hot cream, then pour the egg mixture into the saucepan and continue cooking over medium-low heat, using a heatproof spatula. Stir slowly until thickened (to coat the back of a spoon).

REMOVE FROM HEAT and pour through a strainer into another container placed over an ice bath. Add vanilla and stir often to cool. Cover with plastic wrap and allow to cool completely. Sauce is ready after chilling and will last in the refrigerator up to 1 week.

CALIFORNIA WINE CELLAR

Like we mentioned in the

the introduction, when pairing pizza with wine, pair according to the pizza toppings.

A good rule of thumb to remember is that relatively simple, fruit-driven, soft-textured wines—red or white—usually do best with pizza. To help you out, we paired all of the pizza recipes for you, but feel free to experiment as everyone's palate is different. Here are some more general guidelines to consider. If you have a hankering for a tomato-laden pizza, pop the cork on a Cabernet Franc. For cheese pizzas, try a Barbera, Sangiovese, or Zinfandel. Zins also pair very nicely with sausage pizzas. For pepperoni lovers and pies loaded

with vegetables, a fine Chianti will do the trick. For white sauce pizzas, a crisp Chardonnay will complement well, as would a fruity Pinot Noir.

We hope this book will inspire you to create new pizzas and try new wines. And that's a good thing, as the fun is in the testing. All of the wineries featured in this book are listed in the following pages. Go ahead and contact them directly to learn more about a particular wine, or wine in general.

Alexander & Wayne
2922 Grand Avenue
Los Olivos, CA 93441
(805) 688-9665; (800) 824-8584
www.alexanderandwayne.com

Arbios Cellars
561 Mission Boulevard
Santa Rosa, CA 95409
(707) 539-5641
www.PraxisCellars.com

Arthur Earl
2921 Grand Avenue
Los Olivos, CA 93441
(805) 693-1771; (800) 646-3275
www.arthurearl.com

Artiste
3569 Sagunto Street, Studio 102
Santa Ynez, CA 93460
(805) 686-2626
www.artiste.com

Buttonwood Farm Winery & Vineyard
1500 Alamo Pintado
Solvang, CA 93463
(805) 688-3032
www.buttonwoodwinery.com

Byron Wines
5250 Tepusquet Road
Santa Maria, CA 93454
(805) 686-2626
www.byronwines.com

Cambria Estate Winery
5475 Chardonnay Lane
Santa Maria, CA 93454
(888) 339-9463
www.cambriawines.com

Carhartt Vineyard
2990-A Grand Avenue
Los Olivos, CA 93441
(805) 693-5100
www.carharttvineyard.com

Castoro Cellars
1315 North Bethel Road
Templeton, CA 93465
(805) 238-0725; (888) DAM-FINE
www.castorocellars.com

Consilience
2933 Grand Avenue
Los Olivos, CA 93441
(805) 691-1020
www.consilience.com

Curtis Winery
5249 Foxen Canyon Road
Los Olivos, CA 93441
(805) 686-8999
www.curtiswinery.com

Dog Hill Vineyard
P.O. Box 106
Santa Ynez, CA 93460
www.doghillvineyard.com

Dry Creek Vineyard
3770 Lambert Bridge Road
Healdsburg, CA 95448
(800) 864-9463
www.drycreekvineyard.com

EOS Estate Winery
5625 Highway 46 East
Paso Robles, CA 93446
(805) 239-2562
www.eosvintage.com

Falcone Family Vineyards
1902 Ballard Canyon Road
Solvang, CA 93463
(805) 686-9545
www.falconefamilyvineyards.com

Fiore Wine Company
P.O. Box 838
Santa Ynez, CA 93460
(888) 705-2010
www.sognodelfiore.com

Firestone Vineyard
5000 Zaca Station Road
Los Olivos, CA 93441
(805) 688-3940
www.firestonewine.com

Foley Estates Vineyard & Winery
6121 East Highway 246
Lompoc, CA 93436
(805) 737-6222
www.foleywines.com

Foppiano Vineyards
P.O. Box 606
Healdsburg, CA 95448
(707) 433-7272
www.foppiano.com

Fulcrum Wines
East Coast Sales Office
116 Sears Avenue
Atlantic Highlands, NJ 07717
(732) 610-9602
www.fulcrumwines.com

Gainey Vineyards
3950 East Highway 246
Santa Ynez, CA 93460
(805) 688-0558
www.gaineyvineyard.com

Great Oaks Ranch & Vineyard
2450 Calzada Avenue
Santa Ynez, CA 93460
(805) 686-0895
www.greatoaksranch.com

Io
5250 Tepusquet Road
Santa Maria, CA 93454
(805) 934-4770
www.iowines.com

Jalama Vineyard
P.O. Box 3004
Lompoc, CA 93438
(805) 588-9768
www.jalamavineyard.com

Kinton Wines
5475 Chardonnay Lane
Santa Maria, CA 93454
(866) 372-5333
www.kintonwines.com

Koehler Winery
5360 Foxen Canyon Road
Los Olivos, CA 93441
(805) 693-8384
www.koehlerwinery.com

Kynsi
2212 Corbett Canyon Road
Arroyo Grande, CA 93420
(805) 544-8461
www.kynsi.com

Lincourt Vineyards
1711 Alamo Pintado Road
Solvang, CA 93463
(805) 688-8554
www.lincourtwines.com

Lucas & Lewellen Vineyards
1645 Copenhagen Drive
Solvang, CA 93463
(805) 686-9336
www.llwine.com

Mandolina Wines
1665 Copenhagen Drive
Solvang, CA 93463
(805) 686-5506; (888) 777-6663
www.mandolinawines.com

Mauritson Family Winery
2859 Dry Creek Road
Healdsburg, CA 95448
(707) 431-0804
www.mauritsonwines.com

Melville Winery
5185 East Highway 246
Lompoc, CA 93436
(805) 735-7030
www.melvillewinery.com

Monticello Vineyards
Corley Family Napa Valley
4242 Big Ranch Road
Napa, CA 94558
(707) 253-2802
www.CorleyFamilyNapaValley.com

Palmina Wines
1520 East Chestnut Court
Lompoc, CA 93436
(805) 735-2030
www.palminawines.com

Paraiso Vineyards
37500 Foothill Road
Soledad, CA 93960
(831) 678-0300
www.ParaisoVineyards.com

Robert Hall Winery
3443 Mill Road
Paso Robles, CA 93446
(805) 239-1616
www.roberthallwinery.com

Rusack Vineyards
1819 Ballard Canyon Road
Solvang, CA 93463
(805) 688-1278
www.rusackvineyards.com

Sunstone Vineyards & Winery
125 Refugio Road
Santa Ynez, CA 93460
(805) 688-9463
www.sunstonewinery.com

Tablas Creek Vineyard
9339 Adelaida Road
Paso Robles, CA 93446
(805) 237-1231
www.tablascreek.com

Tre Anelli
2923 Grand Avenue
Los Olivos, CA 93441
(805) 686-3000
www.treanelliwine.com

Wildhurst Vineyards
3855 Main Street
P.O. Box 1310
Kelseyville, CA 95451
(800) 595-WINE (9463)
www.wildhurst.com

ACKNOWLEDGMENTS

Chef Leonardo Curti and author James O. Fraioli would like to personally thank the following individuals for their generous assistance and support with this book:

Andrea Mugnaini
Mugnaini Wood-Fired Ovens
11 Hangar Way
Watsonville, California 95076
Toll Free: 888.887.7206; Phone: 831.761.1767
www.mugnaini.com

Montgomery Miller & Bill Robbins

Jeff Trujillo
Ed's Kasilof Seafoods
www.kasilofseafoods.com

Ellen Roberts
Stolt Sea Farm/Sterling Caviar
www.sterlingcaviar.com

The authors would also like to give thanks to:

Gibbs Smith and Gibbs Smith, Publisher; Andrea Hurst and Andrea Hurst Literary Management; designer Debra McQuiston; Rex Browning; photographers Jessica Nicosia-Nadler and Meagan Szasz; Brooks Institute of Photography; Trattoria Grappolo and the community of Santa Ynez Valley; Tim and Susan Gorham; Jeff and Janet Olsson; Consilience Wines and Tre Anelli; Gainey Vineyard; Roblar Winery; Sunstone Winery; Melanie Hill and Weber (www.weber.com); Santa Ynez Stone and Tile; Alfonso and Giorgio Curti; Jennifer, Sophia, Isabella, and Camilla Curti; Luigi Antonio Curti and Maria Santoro; Linda Vathayanon; Cindy Fraioli; Rachelle and Tish; Jim, Karin, and Tanya Fraioli; and all the participating wineries, which were a pleasure to work with.

Meet Our Photographers

Chef Leonardo Curti and author James O. Fraioli discovered Jessica and Meagan, two talented photographers, during a Brooks Institute of Photography photo shoot at Leonardo's restaurant, Trattoria Grappolo. So impressed with their work, Curti and Fraioli invited them back to photograph *Pizza & Wine*.

Jessica Nicosia-Nadler is a young accomplished photographer born and raised in Long Island, New York. After studying abroad in Florence, Italy, a deep passion for photography emerged, leading her to world-renowned Brooks Institute of Photography in Santa Barbara, California. Earning a B.A. in Professional Photography with a concentration in Food and Product Advertising Photography, Jessica's talents are recognized and applauded today by some of the most influential people in the world of photography. Jessica admits her passion is for all things Italian—the language, food, wine, and the country itself—which inspires her unique photographic style. Jessica and her husband, David, currently reside in Ventura, California. Visit her on the web at www.jessicanicosia.com.

Meagan Szasz is an aspiring young photographer. Born and raised in Traverse City, Michigan, she fell in love with photography at an early age. While attending the prestigious Brooks Institute of Photography in Santa Barbara, California, she learned the fundamentals of becoming a professional photographer. More importantly, she discovered a passion for combining her love of food with her love of photography. Meagan currently resides in Los Angeles, California. Please visit her on the web at www.mszasz.com.

FOOD INDEX

METRIC CONVERSION CHART

Liquid and Dry Measures

U.S.	Canadian	Australian
1/4 teaspoon	1 mL	1 ml
1/2 teaspoon	2 mL	2 ml
1 teaspoon	5 mL	5 ml
1 tablespoon	15 mL	20 ml
1/4 cup	50 mL	60 ml
1/3 cup	75 mL	80 ml
1/2 cup	125 mL	125 ml
2/3 cup	150 mL	170 ml
3/4 cup	175 mL	190 ml
1 cup	250 mL	250 ml
1 quart	1 liter	1 litre

Temperature Conversion Chart

Fahrenheit	Celsius
250	120
275	140
300	150
325	160
350	180
375	190
400	200
425	220
450	230
475	240
500	260

WINE INDEX